Bermuda

WORLD BIBLIOGRAPHICAL SERIES

General Editors:
Robert G. Neville (Executive Editor)
John J. Horton

Robert A. Myers   Hans H. Wellisch
Ian Wallace   Ralph Lee Woodward, Jr.

John J. Horton is Deputy Librarian of the University of Bradford and was formerly Chairman of its Academic Board of Studies in Social Sciences. He has maintained a longstanding interest in the discipline of area studies and its associated bibliographical problems, with special reference to European Studies. In particular he has published in the field of Icelandic and of Yugoslav studies, including the two relevant volumes in the World Bibliographical Series.

Robert A. Myers is Associate Professor of Anthropology in the Division of Social Sciences and Director of Study Abroad Programs at Alfred University, Alfred, New York. He has studied post-colonial island nations of the Caribbean and has spent two years in Nigeria on a Fulbright Lectureship. His interests include international public health, historical anthropology and developing societies. In addition to *Amerindians of the Lesser Antilles: a bibliography* (1981), *A Resource Guide to Dominica, 1493-1986* (1987) and numerous articles, he has compiled the World Bibliographical Series volumes on *Dominica* (1987), *Nigeria* (1989) and *Ghana* (1991).

Ian Wallace is Professor of German at the University of Bath. A graduate of Oxford in French and German, he also studied in Tübingen, Heidelberg and Lausanne before taking teaching posts at universities in the USA, Scotland and England. He specializes in contemporary German affairs, especially literature and culture, on which he has published numerous articles and books. In 1979 he founded the journal *GDR Monitor*, which he continues to edit under its new title *German Monitor*.

Hans H. Wellisch is Professor emeritus at the College of Library and Information Services, University of Maryland. He was President of the American Society of Indexers and was a member of the International Federation for Documentation. He is the author of numerous articles and several books on indexing and abstracting, and has published *The Conversion of Scripts and Indexing and Abstracting: an International Bibliography*, and *Indexing from A to Z*. He also contributes frequently to *Journal of the American Society for Information Science*, *The Indexer* and other professional journals.

Ralph Lee Woodward, Jr. is Professor of History at Tulane University, New Orleans. He is the author of *Central America, a Nation Divided*, 2nd ed. (1985), as well as several monographs and more than seventy scholarly articles on modern Latin America. He has also compiled volumes in the World Bibliographical Series on *Belize* (1980), *El Salvador* (1988), *Guatemala* (Rev. Ed.) (1992) and *Nicaragua* (Rev. Ed.) (1994). Dr. Woodward edited the Central American section of the *Research Guide to Central America and the Caribbean* (1985) and is currently associate editor of Scribner's *Encyclopedia of Latin American History*.

VOLUME 205

Bermuda

Paul G. Boultbee
and
David F. Raine

Compilers

CLIO PRESS

OXFORD, ENGLAND · SANTA BARBARA, CALIFORNIA
DENVER, COLORADO

© Copyright 1998 by ABC-CLIO Ltd.

British Library Cataloguing in Publication Data

Boultbee, Paul G.
Bermuda. – (World bibliographical series; v. 205)
1. Bermuda Islands – Bibliography
I. Title   II. Raine, David F.
016.9′7299

ISBN 1–85109–170–X

ABC-CLIO Ltd.,
Old Clarendon Ironworks,
35A Great Clarendon Street,
Oxford OX2 6AT, England.

ABC-CLIO Inc.,
130 Cremona Drive,
Santa Barbara,
CA 93117, USA.

Designed by Bernard Crossland.
Typeset by Columns Design Ltd., Reading, England.
Printed and bound in Great Britain by Bookcraft (Bath) Ltd., Midsomer Norton.

THE WORLD BIBLIOGRAPHICAL SERIES

This series, which is principally designed for the English speaker, will eventually cover every country (and some of the world's principal regions and cities), each in a separate volume comprising annotated entries on works dealing with its history, geography, economy and politics; and with its people, their culture, customs, religion and social organization. Attention will also be paid to current living conditions – housing, education, newspapers, clothing, etc. – that are all too often ignored in standard bibliographies; and to those particular aspects relevant to individual countries. Each volume seeks to achieve, by use of careful selectivity and critical assessment of the literature, an expression of the country and an appreciation of its nature and national aspirations, to guide the reader towards an understanding of its importance. The keynote of the series is to provide, in a uniform format, an interpretation of each country that will express its culture, its place in the world, and the qualities and background that make it unique. The views expressed in individual volumes, however, are not necessarily those of the publisher.

VOLUMES IN THE SERIES

*To Budge and Alan
with love and respect*

PGB

*To my wife, artist Jill Amos Raine,
whose sensitive watercolours succeed,
where the written word fails*

DFR

Contents

Contents

Introduction

Bermuda, situated in the Atlantic Ocean about 650 miles east of North Carolina and about 775 miles southeast of New York City, enjoys a subtropical climate. A fishhook-shaped chain of approximately 150 islands composed of coral, limestone and fossilized sand dunes, the country sits on the summit of a long-extinct volcano. Its islands, the largest of which are linked by bridges, stretch for twenty-one miles in length and rarely exceed much more than one mile in width.

Bermuda was first discovered in 1503 by Juan de Bermudez, the Spanish captain of *La Garza*, and appeared on maps of the region as early as 1511. However, although discovered by the Spanish and frequented by shipwrecked Portuguese, French and English mariners, Bermuda was not settled for another century. In May 1609, a fleet of nine ships under the command of Admiral Sir George Somers sailed from England en route to Jamestown, Virginia. Off the coast of St. George's Island, Somers' ship, *Sea Venture*, ran aground with 150 crew and passengers. For nine months they lived on the island while two new ships, *Patience* and *Deliverance*, were constructed from the wreckage and local cedar trees in order that the aborted voyage might continue. Two crew members were left behind, including Christopher Carter who became Bermuda's first permanent settler and who remained until his death.

Shortly after the Somers party finally arrived at Jamestown, reports of the wreck of the *Sea Venture* appeared in England. These reports, said to be the basis for William Shakespeare's *The Tempest*, soon prompted the English parliament to encourage settlement of the islands through the Virginia Company. In 1612, under the leadership of the colony's first governor, Richard Moore, a master ship's carpenter, fifty permanent settlers arrived from England and the town of St. George's, Bermuda's first capital, was founded. (It remained the capital until 1815 when the House of Assembly was moved to Hamilton.) By 1615, the Somers Island Company was granted a charter to govern the islands in accordance with English law and, in 1620, the first government assembly was held. In 1684, following years of disastrous economic policy and mismanagement, the Somers Island Company lost its charter and was dissolved. Subsequently, Bermuda became a Crown Colony.

By the outset of the American War of Independence (1775-83), the population of more than 10,000 had become quite dependent on the American colonies. Far from England, the island was not fertile enough to sustain an appropriate agricultural industry. Thus, Bermudians were torn between their loyalty to the Crown and their need to remain on good terms with their fellow colonists. In 1775, for example, an American trade blockade potentially threatened the island with starvation. As a result, Bermudians raided a large gunpowder magazine in St. George's and stole 100 barrels of gunpowder which were transported to a couple of American brigantines anchored offshore. In this instance, Bermudians had felt forced to give General George Washington the gunpowder in return for lifting the blockade.

Following American independence, Bermuda became a very important link in Britain's world-wide empire. In 1809 construction of the Royal Naval Dockyard began, using English convicts who were housed in hulk ships at Grassy Bay. This strategic military defence became the regional headquarters for the Royal Navy fleet and administration. In 1814, for example, it was the staging port for the British fleet's attack on Washington, DC during the War of 1812 (1812-14).

In the 1860s, Bermuda played yet another role in an American conflict when St. George's became a major centre of trade between the Confederacy and Europe during the American Civil War (1861-65). Blockade runners plying the waters between Bermuda and the Southern ports ran goods en route to Europe to Bermuda in exchange for guns and ammunition.

After this flurry of economic activity, the war ended and Bermuda's economy suffered badly. The island's economy during the 17th and 18th centuries had been based primarily on shipbuilding, tobacco cultivation and export, whaling, fishing and the salt trade from the Turks and Caicos Islands, then a Bermudian colony. By the late 19th century, however, these industries had run their course and Bermuda desperately needed economic revitalization.

Two new directions helped ease Bermuda's troubles. First, at the end of the 19th century and the beginning of the 20th century, the cultivation of Bermuda onions, potatoes, and Easter lilies developed into a significant agricultural industry. Unfortunately, by the mid-1950s, agriculture had declined dramatically. On the other hand, tourism became a second economic force after the late 1920s and continues to bring prosperity to Bermuda. Over 500,000 people visit the country each year and tourism accounts for a significant amount of all employment, directly and indirectly.

By the mid-20th century, a third force began to play a major role in Bermuda's economic development. An important commercial and 'offshore' financial sector has made Bermuda one of the world's leading insurance markets with more than 8,000 exempted companies registered in the country. Although it is almost entirely dependent upon imports, Bermuda does have, for its size, a significant export business in rum, flowers, and medicinal and pharmaceutical products. Bermuda has also become a centre for the 'free-flag' registration of shipping, giving it the fifth largest such fleet in the world.

Bermuda, which is divided into nine parishes and two municipalities, is a dependent territory of the United Kingdom and the oldest self-governing colony in the British Commonwealth. It was given complete autonomy over local affairs by the Constitution introduced in 1968, although the Crown continues to be responsible for external affairs and matters of security. Universal adult suffrage was established in 1963, the same year in which Bermuda's first political party, the Progressive Labour Party (PLP), was established. The United Bermuda Party (UBP) was formed in the following year, and the National Liberal Party (NLP) appeared in 1985, organized by disenchanted members of the PLP.

In the latter half of the 20th century the question of independence from Great Britain has taken the occasional political spotlight. The PLP continues to campaign for independence while the UBP, which has formed the government since the party's inception, supports a generally more dependent status. A 1978 Royal Commission recommended early independence for Bermuda, but the majority of the population at the time did not support this proposal. Furthermore, in a referendum on independence held in August 1995, independence was opposed by 74.1 per cent of voters, while only 25.9 per cent supported it.

Whether or not Bermuda becomes an independent nation, the House of Assembly, one of the oldest parliaments in the world, will, for the foreseeable future, continue to promote Bermuda as a haven for tourists and an international business centre.

The bibliography

Although selective, this bibliography does identify those books, periodical articles, magazines and newspapers which collectively provide a very thorough source of information about Bermuda. The 545 entries have been grouped into thirty-seven categories, with sub-categories, which are similar to those found in other volumes of the World Bibliographical Series. Despite its potential interest for some readers, a separate section on the enigmatic Bermuda Triangle has not been included. Because few current materials are readily available and the subject is so specialized, individual entries on the topic have been limited to two bibliographies.

All sections are arranged with the most recently published items listed first. Two or more items published in the same year have been listed alphabetically by the first major word in the title. Books and periodical articles have been listed together with government documents. Individual theses and dissertations have not been included.

Most of the items listed in this bibliography can be found in major academic and large public library collections in North America and Great Britain. However, many of the items have been published in Bermuda and some may not always be readily available outside the country. They are available at The Bermuda Library (13 Queen Street, Hamilton HM 11, Bermuda).

Acknowledgements

I would like to thank all those individuals who have helped me to prepare this bibliography. Grace Rawlins, Head Librarian at the Bermuda Library, and her reference staff made me most welcome and gave generous help with my research needs during my stay in Bermuda. I am particularly grateful to Rosalie Bachor and Bonnie Hawley, staff members of the Red Deer College Library, who were diligent in assisting me with many interlibrary loans. Thanks are also due to Maureen Toews of the Red Deer College Library who shared her office with me while I was on leave, thereby allowing me on-line access to library catalogues world-wide.

As always, I thank my wife Glynis who continues to support and encourage my bibliographic research.

Paul G. Boultbee
December 1997

During the last thirty years, a succession of Bermudian librarians has made an indelible contribution towards the collection and preservation of Bermudian literature: Mrs Terry Tucker, Miss Helen Rowe, Mr Cyril Packwood, and Ms Grace Rawlins. A considerable debt of gratitude is owed to each of them, and their staffs, for their devotion to preserving the written word.

David F. Raine
December 1997

The Country and Its People

1 Bermuda shorts: the hidden side of the richest place on earth.
T. C. Sobey.   New York: Barricade Books, 1996. 335p. bibliog.
Over 300 newspaper articles and letters to the editor from the *Royal Gazette* (see item
no. 522) provide 'revealing peeks at how the unusual, insulated [Bermudian] society
works'. The book covers the period 1982-95, and also includes fifteen editorial
cartoons by Peter Woolcock. This amusing view of Bermudian society of the late 20th
century should be compared with William Zuill's *Bermuda sampler* (see item no. 27).

2 Triumph of the spirit: heroes and heroines, Bermuda role models.
Edited by Dale Butler.   Warwick, Bermuda: The Writers' Machine,
1995. 167p. (Jacks Series).
The short biographies in this volume highlight ten accomplished Bermudians who
have helped to shape Bermuda's history in the 20th century: marathon runner Stanley
Burgess (1901-84); musician Lance Hayward (d. 1991); teachers Edith Crawford
(1880-1978), Louisa Gardiner Richards (1905-92), Kenneth Ellsworth Robinson
(1911-78), Rosalie Pearman-Smith (1896-1980), Charles Cecil Snaith (1897-1977)
and Katie Tankard (1904-86); civil servant Valerie Scott (1931-87); and businessman
John G. Bassett (1901-90).

3 Your Bermuda: all you need to know about our island home.
George Rushe.   Hamilton, Bermuda: Published by the Author, 1995.
206p.
This very handy, encyclopaedic guide to Bermuda is useful to both resident and visitor
alike. Rushe provides information on a multitude of subjects from agriculture to
wrecks. The alphabetic listing contains appropriate cross-references and is
supplemented by an index. There is no map of the island in the book but the work
itself is an extremely valuable item for any Bermuda collection. *Your Bermuda* is the
successor to *Bermuda: as a matter of fact*, which was first published in 1959 by the
Altrusa Club of Bermuda.

4 **Bermuda.**
Edited by Martha Ellen Zenfell.   Boston, Massachusetts: Houghton
Mifflin; Singapore: APA Productions, 1994. 301p. 4 maps. bibliog.
(Insight Guide Series, vol. 217).

This excellent guide to Bermuda includes articles written by well-known Bermudian
authors covering architecture, festivals, sailing, sports, visual arts, calypso, food, flora
and fauna, and the Bermuda Triangle. There are also sections on Hamilton, West End
and East End, Harrington Sound, and the small islands. A small section provides
travel tips. The colour photographs which accompany the text are arguably the
highlight of the work.

5 **Tea with Tracey: the woman's survival guide to Bermuda.**
Tracey Caswell.   Hamilton, Bermuda: Print Link, 1994. 143p.

Caswell takes a humourous approach to dispensing practical advice on coping with
everyday living in Bermuda. Her topics include climate, cleaning, social customs,
food, holidays, transport, flora and fauna, insects and personal hygiene. This informal,
but informative, book is designed for new residents or long-term visitors.

6 **Faces of Bermuda volume II.**
John Weatherhill.   Warminster, England: Morrell Wylye Head, 1991.
144p.

Similar to Weatherhill's first *Faces of Bermuda* (see item no. 10), this unique social
document presents 115 black-and-white portraits of a variety of Bermudians,
including the island's archivist, journalists, children and students, politicians,
teachers, lawyers and a butler. An index provides a biographical sketch of each person.

7 **The back yard: a Bermuda childhood.**
Ann Zuill Williams.   London: Macmillan Caribbean, 1988. 85p. 2 maps.

Williams was born in 1935 and belongs to old Bermuda families on both her maternal
and paternal side. Her childhood memories provide a fascinating view of Bermuda
from 1939 to 1945 and a glimpse of a graceful and carefree life at the family home,
Orange Grove, parts of which date to 1650.

8 **Bermuda.**
John J. Jackson.   London: David & Charles; New York: Hippocrene
Books, 1988. 208p. 6 maps. bibliog. (Islands Series).

This work, written for the general reader who wants more detail than can be found in a
typical tourist guide, includes information on geology and geography, history, the
people and social customs, government and politics, the economy, tourism and the
island's future prospects.

9 **Images of Bermuda.**
Roger LaBrucherie.   Pine Valley, California: Imagenes Press, 1987.
106p. 4 maps.

This work tells Bermuda's story through 112 wonderful colour photographs depicting
Bermuda's history and heritage, natural resources, people and architecture. There is no
text but the captions for each photograph are informative.

10   **Faces of Bermuda.**
      John Weatherhill.   Warminster, England: Morrell Wylye Head, 1985.
      136p.

Weatherhill's 118 black-and-white portraits present a good historic record of Bermudians from all walks of society. His work includes a lighthouse keeper, the Chief Justice, artists, teachers, the Speaker of the House of Assembly and a variety of others. Each individual is identified by name and discussed in a brief biographical sketch in an index. Weatherhill produced another volume in 1991 (see item no. 6).

11   **South America, Central America, and the Caribbean.**
      London: Europa Publications, 1985- . biennial.

This excellent quick-reference book covers all countries in South and Central America, and the Caribbean including Bermuda. Articles provide background material on the region and material on regional organizations. Entries for each country include statistics as well as information on history, politics and government, religion, the media, finance and banking, trade and industry, tourism and education. The entry for Bermuda is brief, but constitutes a useful overview.

12   **Bermuda report, 1972-79- .**
      Bermuda. Department of Information Services.   Hamilton, Bermuda:
      The Department, 1981- . irregular.

This official government handbook has appeared in three editions to date: *Bermuda report 1972-79*, *Bermuda report 1980-1984*, and *Bermuda report 1985-1988*. Contents include information on the government and administration, the financial system and the economy, law and order, manpower and immigration, education, community and cultural affairs, religion, sports and recreation, health and social services, public works and utilities, transport and communications, tourism, agriculture and fisheries, housing and land use, and military installations. There is also a section of statistics. *Bermuda report* continues the annual Foreign and Commonwealth Office reports published in London from the late 1800s up to 1971.

13   **Bermuda: a new study.**
      Gilbert J. Butland.   New York: Vantage Press, 1980. 161p. 5 maps.
      bibliog.

In this well-researched and documented work, Butland examines the changes which have taken place in Bermuda since 1959. As well as giving background information on geography and history, he also looks at the tourist industry, agriculture and fisheries, communications, the social environment and the economic structure. Although now dated, this book could provide useful background information for current research. There are thirty-two black-and-white photographs.

14   **Heritage.**
      Kenneth Ellsworth Robinson.   London: Macmillan, 1979. 320p.

This account of the foundation upon which the present black Bermudian heritage has grown was published by Macmillan for The Berkeley Educational Society in Bermuda. Robinson discusses social, educational, political, intellectual and economic activities and events for the first twenty-five years after emancipation (1834-59). This work represents the first of a proposed four volumes covering the century following

3

emancipation. However, the author died in October 1978 and the series remains incomplete.

15 Caribbean Year Book.
Toronto: Caribook, 1977/78- . annual.

First published in 1926/27 under the title, *Year book of the West Indies and Countries of the Caribbean*. In 1953 the title was changed to *West Indies and Caribbean Year Book*. It is a very good quick-reference book for Bermuda as well as for all other countries in the Caribbean area. It includes information on history, climate, population, religion, government, public and social services, public utilities, communications, natural resources, industry, finance, and travel and tourism. There is also a business directory.

16 Bermuda hodge podge: a bedtime book.
Sister Jean de Chantal Kennedy. Hamilton, Bermuda: Bermuda Book Stores, 1975. 143p. map.

This collection of tales, anecdotes and facts has been gathered by the author over a twenty-five-year period. It contains a variety of pieces on such topics as cookery, folklore, education, hurricanes, geography, shipwrecks, history, law, herbal medicine, blockade running, slavery, shipping and religion. There is no table of contents and no particular order to the essays, but there is a useful index.

17 Bermuda: balmy, British and beautiful.
Peter Benchley. *National Geographic Magazine*, vol. 140, no. 1 (July 1971), p. 93-121.

After providing a brief historical synopsis, Benchley discusses shipwrecks and salvaging, shipbuilding and sailing, and the environmental work of naturalist David Wingate.

18 Bermuda in full color.
Hans W. Hannau. Garden City, New York: Doubleday, 1970. 128p. 3 maps.

Contains information on history, geology, climate, vegetation and sightseeing. However, the real highlight of this book is the ninety-six colour plates. The book was also released in 1971 under the title *Bermuda in full colour* (London: Hale) and in 1972 under the title *The Bermuda isles in full color* (New York: Hastings House).

19 Bermuda: the summer islands.
Anne Bolt. *Geographical Magazine*, vol. 31, no. 12 (April 1959), p. 587-97.

In this well-illustrated article, Bolt touches on history, geology, climate, agriculture, the economy, architecture and tourism.

20 **Bermuda copes with major problems.**
Marcus Van Steen. *Canadian Geographical Journal*, vol. 56, no. 1
(Jan. 1958), p. 27-35.

Van Steen outlines several major problems faced by Bermuda in the past 150 years:
the introduction in 1859 of the Mediterranean fruit fly which had wiped out the
island's fruit export business by 1901; the end of the great days of sail in the late 19th
century; the unfavourable North American tariff legislation of 1891, 1930 and 1936;
the Second World War's effect on the tourist trade and import food shipments; the
introduction in 1944 of scale infestation which left ninety per cent of the island's
cedar trees bare and dead within ten years; the population growth of the 20th century;
and water supply problems. Van Steen then discusses how Bermudians have coped
with these problems and what their future strategies might be.

21 **Bermuda, cradled in warm seas.**
Beverley M. Bowie. *National Geographic Magazine*, vol. 105, no. 2
(Feb. 1954), p. 203-38.

Describing Bermuda as an attractive tourist destination, Bowie highlights the
Bermudian way of life. She provides information on history, the judicial system,
population trends, the impact of the Second World War on communications, and the
successful efforts to save the cahow bird from extinction.

22 **Bermuda through the camera of James B. Heyl, 1868-1897:**
a newspaper record, illustrated by photographs of Bermuda's
ever-changing scenes.
Compiled by Edith Stowe Godfrey Heyl.   Hamilton, Bermuda:
Bermuda Book Stores, 1951. 240p.

James Bell Heyl was a Bermudian pharmacist and avid photographer. This collection
of 125 black-and-white photographs documents Bermuda in the late 19th century.
Topics illustrated include landscapes, seascapes, the Dockyard, ships and the military.
There are also major sections on religion and churches (p. 59-89) and domestic
architecture (p. 91-121). Edith Heyl's text is a useful adjunct to her father's
photographs. This valuable photographic record was produced in an edition limited to
1,500 copies.

23 **Bermuda journey: a leisurely guidebook.**
William Edward Sears Zuill.   New York: Coward-McCann, 1946.
426p. 10 maps. bibliog.

The main body of this work takes the form of a detailed guide along the highways and
byways of Bermuda. As part of this guided tour, the author, a well-respected local
writer and historian, provides a great deal of factual information and a number of
anecdotes and Bermudian stories. This volume is essential to any Bermuda collection.

24 **Bermudiana.**
Ronald John Williams.   New York: Rinehart, 1946. 256p.

The ten sections of this book, amply illustrated with 236 black-and-white photographs
by Walter Rutherford, cover history, ships and sailors, the land, architecture, the
shore, yacht racing, Bermuda as a health resort and playground, the government,

Bermuda at mid-century, and approaching Bermuda by sea and air. Williams provides a wonderful view of Bermuda as it was at the time of writing.

25 Happy landing in Bermuda.

Edward John Long. *National Geographic Magazine*, vol. 75, no. 2 (Feb. 1939), p. 213-38.

Writing at a time when Bermuda was just beginning to attract large numbers of tourists, Long suggests that Bermuda is an ideal place to visit or to live. He discusses the island's history, attractions and social conditions. Fourteen excellent black-and-white photographs and twelve fair colour photographs are included. This pre-Second World War article is a good complement to Bowie's 1954 *National Geographic* article (see item no. 21).

26 The Bermudas: impressions of a Canadian.

Gordon M. Dallyn. *Canadian Geographical Journal*, vol. 17, no. 5 (Nov. 1938), p. 216-39.

This general introduction discusses the geology, history, climate and commerce of Bermuda. Dallyn provides a good overview of the island from an outsider's point of view. Thirty-six black-and-white photographs accompany the text which begins on p. 217.

27 Bermuda sampler 1815-1850: being a collection of newspaper items, extracts from books and private papers, together with many explanatory notes and a variety of illustrations.

William Edward Sears Zuill. Hamilton, Bermuda: Bermuda Book Stores, 1937. 456p. map.

These 626 extracts are presented in chronological order and are taken almost entirely from the *Bermuda Gazette* and the *Royal Gazette* (see item no. 522). Topics include politics, entertainment, shipping, wrecks, fashion, personalities, society, deaths, crime and education. The work provides a fascinating view of early 19th-century Bermuda.

28 Bermuda in three colors.

Carveth Wells. New York: Robert McBride, 1935. 271p. bibliog.

Wells' work, originally released as a guidebook, is in fact a descriptive account of Bermuda up to the 1930s. The book contains sections on history, geography and geology, as well as information helpful to the 1930s tourist.

29 Bermuda past and present.

Walter Brownell Hayward. New York: Dodd, Mead, 1933. 2nd rev. and enl. ed. 276p. map.

This volume, first published in 1910 (New York: Dodd, Mead) and first revised in 1923 (New York: Dodd, Mead), is primarily an introduction to Bermuda for American visitors. Hayward provides descriptions of the scenery and information on places to visit. However, he also comments in detail on Bermuda's ties with the United States through the Virginia Company in the 17th century, and on the island's involvement in the War of 1812 and the American Civil War. The history sections of the book end with the island's involvement in the First World War. There are sixteen black-and-white photographs.

30 The story of Bermuda.
Hudson Strode. New York: Random House, 1932. 374p.

Despite its age, this book is still a very popular and useful comprehensive introduction to Bermuda. Section I covers Bermuda's history from 1511 to 1865, Bermuda in the early 20th century, and writers who have been associated with Bermuda. Section II provides information on architecture and gardens. The work is illustrated with seventy-five black-and-white photographs by William Rutherford.

31 The islands of Bermuda.
William Howard Taft. *National Geographic Magazine*, vol. 41, no. 1 (Jan. 1922), p. 1-26.

This address, presented before the National Geographic Society in February 1921, is based on Taft's four-week visit to Bermuda in January 1921. He discusses geography, geology, flora and fauna, history and, in particular, government. At the time of writing, there was a suggestion that the United States might purchase the West Indian possessions of Great Britain, including Bermuda, in part settlement of war debts. Taft writes that 'Great Britain would not think of giving up the islands, and the Bermudians would not think of being given up' (p. 26). Fifteen black-and-white photographs and one map accompany the text.

32 Significance of the location of Bermuda.
Robert S. Platt. *Journal of Geography*, vol. 20, no. 1 (Jan. 1921), p. 13-17.

Platt explores the effects of Bermuda's isolated location in the Atlantic Ocean on the development of the island. He suggests that Bermuda's location affected the island's commerce in the 17th and 18th centuries, and contributed to its role in the blockades during the American Civil War. Platt also comments on Bermuda's role as a coaling station, defence outpost and tourist destination.

33 Bermuda.
R. Vashon Rogers. *Queen's Quarterly*, vol. 10, no. 2 (Oct. 1902), p. 125-36.

Provides some background history of the island followed by descriptions of houses, religion and churches, and law and justice. This sympathetic, almost delicate, description is laced with quotations from the Irish poet, Tom Moore.

34 Notes on the Bermudas.
Charles Lawrence Bristol. *Bulletin of the American Geographical Society*, vol. 33, no. 3 (1901), p. 242-48.

In this good, concise, early introduction to Bermuda, Bristol comments on geography and geology, population, industry and agriculture, government, religion, education, and flora and fauna.

Geography

35 The mapping of Bermuda: a bibliography of printed maps and charts 1548-1970.

Margaret Palmer, edited by R. V. Tooley.   Paget, Bermuda: Nicholas Lusher, 1988. 3rd rev. ed. 73p. 41 maps.

A brief introduction and history precede detailed annotations to 125 printed maps dating from 1548 to 1970. The textual information is accompanied by forty-one black-and-white plates. This work was originally published by Palmer under the title *The printed maps of Bermuda* in 1965 (London: Map Collectors' Circle) as number 19 in the Map Collectors' Series. The second edition, under the same title, appeared in 1974.

36 Bermuda mystery waves.

Frederick George Walton Smith.   *Sea Frontiers*, vol. 31, no. 3 (May/June 1985), p. 160-63.

Smith describes mammoth waves, seldom seen in Bermuda, which appeared in the afternoon of 12 November 1984. They occurred every twenty to thirty minutes, lasted for five to ten seconds each and continued for three-and-a-half hours. Smith concludes that they were formed by a storm to the northeast, one thousand miles away. The text appears on p. 162-63, while p. 160-61 consists of a colour photograph of an approaching wave. An unattributed, short follow-up article, 'Source of the Bermuda freak waves' (*Sea Frontiers*, vol. 31, no. 4 [July/Aug. 1985], p. 247), confirms Smith's conjecture and contains a weather map for 11 November 1984 showing the storm system responsible.

37 The islands of Bermuda: each isle and islet's separate story.

Terry Tucker.   Hamilton, Bermuda: Island Press, 1979. 2nd ed. 138p. 4 maps.

In an alphabetical list of the islands which make up Bermuda, Tucker provides geographical, historical and social information. Her comments range from one sentence to several pages. The 120 islands have a total of 173 names; Tucker comments on all of them.

38 Beware the hurricane! the story of the cyclonic tropical storms that have struck Bermuda and the islanders' folk-lore regarding them.

Terry Tucker. Hamilton, Bermuda: Island Press, 1972. 2nd ed. 168p.

Tucker comments on and discusses the major hurricanes and tropical storms that struck Bermuda between 1609 and 1971. She includes newspaper accounts, government reports and information from personal letters and interviews. Her appendices contain an alphabetical list of wrecks off Bermuda with the dates the ships foundered, an explanation of the Beaufort Scale, a list of earthquake shocks that affected Bermuda from 1664 to 1970, and information on the Bermuda Triangle which Tucker classifies with the Loch Ness Monster and flying saucers. *Beware the hurricane!* was first published in 1966 (Hamilton, Bermuda: Hamilton Press).·

39 Hurricanes of the Caribbean and adjacent regions, 1492-1800.

Jose Carlos Millas. Miami, Florida: Academy of the Arts and Sciences of the Americas, 1968. 328p. map. bibliog.

In this fascinating study, Millas examines contemporary documents pertaining to 308 reported hurricanes which allegedly occurred in the Caribbean and adjacent regions between 1492 and 1800. He concludes that forty-five of the reported cases lack sufficient evidence to be considered true hurricanes.

40 The geography of Bermuda.

James Wreford Watson, John Oliver, Catherine H. Foggo. London: Collins, 1965. 128p. 15 maps. bibliog.

This book, prepared under the guidance of the Bermuda Department of Education, was intended for use as a school textbook. It contains information on topography, coastlines, climate, vegetation, soils, occupations, population and settlement. There are twenty-seven photographs as well as numerous diagrams and graphs.

41 The Pleistocene climate of Bermuda.

Kirk Bryan, R. C. Cady. *American Journal of Science*, 5th series, vol. 27, no. 160 (April 1934), p. 241-64.

In an attempt to reconstruct the climate of the Pleistocene in Bermuda, Bryan and Cady discuss the effects of the depressed sea-level and the borders of the ice masses, the Gulf Stream, air temperatures, air pressures and prevailing winds, cyclonic storms and the interglacial periods. They conclude that Bermuda's climate was colder but not too severe, and that wind velocities were higher to the extent that gales prevailed for fifteen to twenty-five per cent of the time. Such conditions were favourable to the dune building so prevalent on the island. They also surmise that interglacial periods were marked by less wind than at present, leading to favourable conditions for soil formation.

42 Hurricanes of the West Indies.

Oliver Lanard Fassig. Washington, DC: Government Printing Office, 1913. 28p. 17 maps. (US Dept. of Agriculture. Weather Bureau. Bulletin X. W. B., 487).

Fassig concentrates on those storms which swept through the Caribbean between 1876 and 1911. He concludes that eighty-eight per cent of hurricanes appear in August, September and October and that they have an average duration of six days. He also provides information on their origins and movements, and pays particular attention to the devastating hurricane of 7-20 August 1899. The maps trace all of the hurricanes under examination.

43 West Indian hurricanes.

Edward Bennett Garriott. Washington, DC: Weather Bureau, 1900. 69p. (US Dept. of Agriculture. Weather Bureau. Bulletin H. W. B., 232).

Reviews the writings of the more prominent meteorologists of the 19th century insofar as they refer to tropical storms of the North Atlantic and presents a chronological list of West Indian storms from 1493 to 1900. There are also descriptions of some of the more important hurricanes.

Geology

General

44   **Origin and community structure of the Harrington Sound notch, Bermuda.**
Martin L. H. Thomas.   *Bulletin of Marine Science*, vol. 58, no. 3 (May 1996), p. 753-63.

The Harrington Sound notch is a deep bioerosional cleft lying just below the mean low tide level and is unique to Harrington Sound. Thomas ascribes the origin of the notch to the boring actions of sponges of the genus Cliona and the bivalve molluscs, Lithohaga. The notch supports a rich epibiota of algae, as well as epifaunal sponges and molluscs. Thomas' work is based on 246 core samples taken from three locations at each of 41 stations located around Harrington Sound.

45   **Terrestrial and shallow marine geology of the Bahamas and Bermuda.**
Edited by H. Allen Curran, Brian White.   Boulder, Colorado: Geological Society of America, 1995. 344p. (Geological Society of America. Special Paper, no. 300).

This collection of twenty-three articles reviews the current knowledge of the geological history of the Bahamas and Bermuda. They were originally presented at the March 1991 symposium, 'Terrestrial and Shallow Marine Geology, Bahamas and Bermuda', which was held in Baltimore, Maryland and sponsored by the Eastern Section of the Society for Sedimentary Geology. Part two of this work contains the five articles which pertain to Bermuda: H. Allen Curran and Brian White, 'Introduction: Bermuda geology' (p. 269); H. L. Vacher, P. J. Hearty and M. P. Rowe, 'Stratigraphy of Bermuda: nomenclature, concepts, and status of multiple systems of classification' (p. 271-94); Dieter Meischner, Rudiger Vollbrecht and Dieter Wehmeyer, 'Pleistocene sea-level yo-yo recorded in stacked beaches, Bermuda South Shore' (p. 295-310); Stanley R. Herwitz and Daniel R. Muhs, 'Bermuda evolution pipe soils: a geochemical evolution of eolian parent materials' (p. 311-23); and John K. Hartsock, Donald L. Woodrow and D. Brooks McKinney, 'Fracture systems in northeastern Bermuda' (p. 325-34).

46   **Quaternary stratigraphy of Bermuda: a high-resolution pre-Sangamonian rock record.**
Paul J. Hearty, H. Leonard Vacher.   *Quaternary Science Reviews*, vol. 13, no. 8 (1994), p. 685-97.

Hearty and Vacher focus on the physical stratigraphy and the ages of pre-Sangamonian deposits (older than 120,000 years) in Bermuda in order to investigate the role that climate plays in the geological record. Carbonate islands like Bermuda are created by climatic changes. Warm climates and high sea levels stimulate carbonate sediment production that result in island growth, while cold glacials expose platforms to weathering, dissolution and soil formation. Bermuda Island Evolution maps (p. 693) show geological changes in Bermuda over the past one million years.

47   **Aminostratigraphy and ages of Pleistocene limestones of Bermuda.**
Paul J. Hearty, H. Leonard Vacher, Richard M. Mitterer.   *Geological Society of America Bulletin*, vol. 104, no. 4 (April 1992), p. 471-80.

The purpose of this paper is to expand the geochronological base for Bermuda using an established physical stratigraphy as an age framework. By developing aminostratigraphies using marine mollusc genera, land snails, and whole-rock samples of bioclastic sand, the authors have been able to gather important information about sea-level history.

48   **Field guide to Pleistocene and modern carbonates of Bermuda.**
Noel P. James, Paul E. Schenk.   Ferry Reach, Bermuda: Bermuda Biological Station for Research, 1983. 72p. bibliog. (Special Publication, no. 25).

Written as a guide for students interested in the origin, deposition, and alteration of carbonate sediments and sedimentary rocks, especially the interactions between organisms and sediments, and early diagenesis. The work is divided into two sections: the nature and origin of the volcanic sea mount and the overlying Pleistocene carbonate rocks; and the sediment, fauna and environments of the Recent rocks. There are forty-five figures scattered throughout the text.

49   **Bermuda sea level during the last interglacial.**
Russel S. Harmon, Lynton S. Land, Richard M. Mitterer, Peter Garrett, Henry P. Schwarcz, Grahame J. Larson.   *Nature*, vol. 289, no. 5797 (5 Feb. 1981), p. 481-83.

The authors have reconstructed a complete record of sea-level fluctuation during the last 70,000 to 135,000 years. This has been done through dating corals, speleothems and molluscs, and through the reinterpretation of geological field relations. The authors have shown that the sea level has ranged from four to six metres above its present level about 125,000 years ago to at least fifteen metres below present levels about 95,000 years ago.

50 **Late Pleistocene sea level history of Bermuda.**
Russel S. Harmon, Henry P. Schwarcz, Derek C. Ford. *Quaternary Research*, vol. 9 (1978), p. 205-18.

The authors present age data for corals and speleothems collected from sixteen metres above to eleven metres below the present sea level. These data provide information on the timing of past glacial events and on the rate of the fall of the sea level during the onset of glaciation. The authors conclude that three major periods of high sea level occurred within the past 200,000 years, and that two longer periods of low sea level separated these high sea-level periods.

51 **Deep Drill 1972: potassium-argon dating of the Bermuda drill core.**
P. H. Reynolds, F. Aumento. *Canadian Journal of Earth Sciences*, vol. 11 (1974), p. 1,269-73.

This study is based on findings from a 767-metre long continuous igneous rock core which was obtained in 1972. Reynolds and Aumento conclude that the sea floor surrounding Bermuda is 110 million years old while the Bermuda seamount itself is considerably younger, closer to 36 million years old.

52 **Coastal dunes of younger Bermuda.**
H. Leonard Vacher. In: *Coastal geomorphology*. Edited by Donald R. Coates. Binghamton, New York: State University of New York, 1973, p. 355-91. bibliog. (Publications in Geomorphology).

Part of the proceedings of the Third Annual Geomorphology Symposia Series held at Binghamton in September 1972. Vacher examines the conditions necessary for the formation of dunes on the external shorelines of Bermuda. He concludes that high sea levels and large volumes of calcarenite were required for their formation while strong winds and gales were also factors in determining their morphology. The article is accompanied by three black-and-white photographs, seven tables, nine maps, eight figures and a bibliography.

53 **Field guide to Bermuda geology.**
Lynton S. Land, Fred T. Mackenzie. St. George's West, Bermuda: Bermuda Biological Station for Research, 1970. 35p. 2 maps. bibliog. (Special Publication, no. 4).

The purpose of this field guide is to acquaint visitors with the geology of Bermuda and to enable scientists to visit the most important localities that have been used to interpret the late Pleistocene history of Bermuda. It is not, however, a complete guide to the stratigraphic areas of Bermuda. The authors provide descriptions of eleven stratigraphic sections throughout the island and seven black-and-white photographs to illustrate several of those sections.

54 **Limestones and red soils of Bermuda.**
G. Blackburn, R. M. Taylor. *Geological Society of America Bulletin*, vol. 80 (Aug. 1969), p. 1,595-98.

Blackburn and Taylor examine the red soils and limestones of Bermuda, as well as the beach sands and submarine clays. They conclude that the development of red clay soils is restricted to the northern parts of the island and the soils were formed when

Quaternary limestones containing volcanic debris were exposed to the elements. In a subsequent discussion piece ('Limestones and red soils of Bermuda: discussion', *Geological Society of America Bulletin*, vol. 81 [Aug. 1970], p. 2,523-24), O. P. Bricker and F. T. Mackenzie reject these general conclusions, question the original observations and provide an alternative hypothesis. Blackburn and Taylor provided their own response ('Limestones and red soils of Bermuda', *Geological Society of America Bulletin*, vol. 81 [Aug. 1970], p. 2,525-26).

55 **Pleistocene history of Bermuda.**
Lynton S. Land, Fred T. Mackenzie, Stephen Jay Gould. *Geological Society of America Bulletin*, vol. 78, no. 8 (Aug. 1967), p. 993-1,006.
Based on three years of co-operative research with particular studies focusing on sedimentation, diagenesis and fossil biota. The authors show the links among Pleistocene rocks and soils (shallow-water, beach and intertidal marine biocalcarenites; eolianites; and red soils) and high sea levels and the interglacial and glacial periods. There is no evidence of Pleistocene tectonism.

56 **Observations on coastal erosion in Bermuda and measurements of the boring rate of the sponge, *Cliona lampa*.**
A. Conrad Neumann. *Limnology and Oceanography*, vol. 11, no. 1 (Jan. 1966), p. 92-108.
Submerged portions of the steep cliffs that ring Harrington Sound are undercut by as much as four to five metres by a notch whose flat roof coincides closely with the level of extreme low tides. Neumann has concluded that bioerosion and not wave action is responsible for this undercutting. Specifically, he has determined that the boring sponge, Cliona lampa, is capable of substrate destruction rates as great as six to seven kilograms per square metre per 100 days. This translates to an erosion rate of one metre of calcarenite per seventy years.

57 **Processes of recent carbonate sedimentation in Harrington Sound, Bermuda.**
A. Conrad Neumann. *Bulletin of Marine Science*, vol. 15, no. 4 (1965), p. 987-1,035.
Harrington Sound, a small, almost entirely enclosed, semi-tropical lagoon, is a nearly ideal carbonate sediment trap. The carbonate sediments which Neumann studied here are largely silt and clay derivatives of the indigenous skeletal biota and surrounding rock.

58 **Bermuda Pleistocene eolianites and paleowinds.**
Fred T. Mackenzie. *Sedimentology*, vol. 3 (1964), p. 52-64.
Mackenzie analyses more than 800 cross-stratified limestones from 129 localities. He concludes that the majority of these limestones appear to be stabilized dunes of the Pleistocene, and the directional features of the dunes suggest paleowind patterns similar to present-day patterns. The majority of the eolianites, composed of wind-borne sand, were formed by onshore winds at times of high sea levels.

59 **Paleosols of Bermuda.**

R. V. Ruhe, J. G. Cady, R. S. Gomez. *Geological Society of America Bulletin*, vol. 72 (Aug. 1961), p. 1,121-42.

The authors' work with soils is based on conclusions reached by Robert Sayles in his 1931 article (see item no. 68). Sayles recognized five buried soils separating eolianites and limestones. He concluded that these paleosols represented interglacial ages or interstadials. Field studies in 1957 and laboratory studies in 1958 and 1959 conducted by Ruhe, Cady and Gomez show that this island-wide correlation may be tenuous. Of the three sites they examined, only one shows all five soils recognized by Sayles. The morphology, physical and chemical properties, and mineralogy of the other two sites show that the soils may represent a major stratigraphic break.

60 **Bermuda: a partially drowned, late mature, Pleistocene karst.**

J. Harlen Bretz. *Bulletin of the Geological Society of America*, vol. 71 (Dec. 1960), p. 1,729-54.

During the Pleistocene era Bermuda repeatedly rose above and fell beneath the surrounding sea. The land was attacked and reduced by rainwater and groundwater. While submerged, the land was renewed by depositions of marine limestones and, when above the water, it received additions of carbonate sand. The soils formed under these conditions have become important stratigraphic markers along with the igneous foundation rocks exposed during times of emergence. Bretz concludes that major karst features appear largely below sea level and must date from times of continental glaciation. He also states that previous writers who concluded that eolian accumulation occurred during Pleistocene low sea-level times, while soil making occurred during times of interglacial high seas, were wrong in their assumptions.

61 **Study of some Bermuda rock.**

Fred Foreman. *Bulletin of the Geological Society of America*, vol. 62 (Nov. 1951), p. 1,297-330.

Foreman describes a petrologic study of subsurface clays and marine limestones from the Castle Harbour area; weathered and water-worn volcanic rock from Gibb's Hill; calcareous soil from the Prospect Military wall; and a conglomerate sample of Hard Bermuda Limestone. Although he cannot determine an age for the clays and marine limestones, Foreman states that they appear to be from the late Tertiary period. There are ten tables and an extensive discussion of chemical, textual and petrographic analyses.

62 **Preglacial history of Bermuda.**

Hilary B. Moore, Doris M. Moore. *Bulletin of the Geological Society of America*, vol. 57 (Feb. 1946), p. 207-22.

Rock from depths up to fifty feet below sea level was taken from the Castle Harbour area and studied for its rich marine fossil content. This represents the record between the post-volcanic period and formations of eolianites in the glacial period. The sequence of fauna and strata evident in the rock indicates a period of the shallowing of the sea. The types of rock described include clay, chert and brick, sandstone, loose sand, shell conglomerates and mangrove peat.

63 **Observations on the structure of Bermuda.**
William Livingston. *Geographical Journal*, vol. 104, no. 1/2
(July-Aug. 1944), p. 40-48.

This detailed examination of the geology of Bermuda is based on Livingston's observations during his tenure as Director of Public Works from September 1929 to July 1938. He pays particular attention to the eolianites and limestones; sand dunes; fossil earths; fossil trees; and fossil eggs and birds' bones. Two maps and nine black-and-white photographs accompany the article.

64 **Bermuda: a product of the ice age.**
C. M. Allen. *Rocks and Minerals*, vol. 15, no. 11 (Nov. 1940),
p. 363-68.

Allen contends that Bermuda is a result of a Tertiary or even pre-Tertiary submarine eruption. He then describes changes in sea level on the original basaltic mountains and the effects of glacial advances and retreats. There are also comments on flora, minerals and caves.

65 **The peat deposits of Bermuda and evidences of postglacial changes in sea-level.**
Arthur S. Knox. *Journal of Geology*, vol. 48, no. 7 (1940), p. 767-80.

In investigating recent submergences of the Bermuda area, Knox undertook a test boring through forty-two feet of the Hamilton or Pembroke marsh. He encountered five layers of woody peat each of which represented periods of relative stability in the sea level. These findings not only offer a means of determining the rate of peat accumulation but also show that sea-level changes were periodic rather than gradual. Since the Hamilton marsh is 97.7 feet deep, Knox surmises that several more woody layers may exist below the forty-two-foot mark.

66 **Minerals from deep sea cores and surface deposits of Bermudian calcareous sediments.**
John A. Young, Jr. *American Journal of Science*, vol. 237, no. 11
(Nov. 1939), p. 798-810.

A report on the minerals found in a set of core samples taken from the sea bottom on the flanks of the Bermuda platform. They have been compared with those found on the island of Bermuda. The samples, which were gathered in 1935, range in depth from 1,320 metres to 3,338 metres. Young discusses the minerals found (quartz, feldspar, hornblende and biotite, pyroxene, glauconite and phillipsite) and speculates on their origins.

67 **Shoal-water deposits of the Bermuda Banks.**
Jean P. Todd. *Journal of Sedimentary Petrology*, vol. 9, no. 1
(April 1939), p. 8-13.

Todd's analyses of the calcareous sediment from the Bermuda Banks show that a correlation does exist between the composition of the sediment and its topographic location. The beach sands are well-sorted and uniform. Lagoon sediment is fine and slightly less well-sorted. The sands of the exposed boundary reef are coarse. The samples used for the study were originally collected in 1934.

68   Bermuda during the ice age.

Robert W. Sayles. *Proceedings of the American Academy of Arts and Sciences*, vol. 66, no. 11 (Nov. 1931), p. 382-467. bibliog.

A valuable geological study of Bermuda. Sayles examines in detail the island's topography, igneous and sedimentary rocks, fossil soils, the region's paleontology, the relationship between petrology and chemistry, and the physiography and evolution of Bermuda. Seventeen figures and a map are included in the text, and thirteen black-and-white plates follow p. 467 on unnumbered pages. There is also an extensive bibliography.

69   Mount Bermuda.

William Beebe. *Atlantic Monthly*, vol. 147 (Feb. 1931), p. 211-15.

In this descriptive narrative, Beebe tries to imagine the volcanic origins of Bermuda and to explain how the first life forms began. The text is based on his research and observations as an underwater marine scientist.

70   Geology of Bermuda Island: the igneous platform.

L. V. Pirsson. *American Journal of Science*, 4th series, vol. 38, no. 225 (Sept. 1914), p. 189-206.

Pirsson discusses and describes forty-eight bore samples taken from scattered sites around Bermuda. He also provides general information on the Bermuda volcano and the composition of the island's rock which is chiefly basaltic lava.

71   Geology of Bermuda Island: petrology of the lavas.

L. V. Pirsson. *American Journal of Science*, 4th series, vol. 38, no. 226 (Oct. 1914), p. 331-44.

In this follow-up to his September 1914 article (see preceding item), Pirsson discusses melilite basalt; lamprophyric lavas; the chemical composition of the lavas; and soils and gravel. He concludes that the lavas consist mainly of melilite basalt with a small amount of trachyte. They have an alkalic character and correspond with lavas of volcanoes that have risen from the ocean floor elsewhere in the Atlantic.

72   The shoal-water deposits of the Bermuda Banks.

Henry B. Bigelow. *Proceedings of the American Academy of Arts and Sciences*, vol. 40 (1905), p. 559-92.

Seventy-six samples of sea-bottom deposits collected during the summers of 1903 and 1904 were examined. The study of these samples of sand sheds light on the method of the growth of a limestone island. Bigelow took his samples from three separate areas: the beaches; the enclosed lagoons; and the shoals and flats inside the boundary reefs. A fourth area between the reefs and the thirty-fathom line is considered but there were no samples from this area available for study. Bigelow found that ninety per cent of the bottom deposits are composed of calcareous material with very little siliceous material evident. The bottom deposits examined were of three main types: blue muds; white marls; and shell sands.

73   **Notes on the geology of the Bermudas.**
     Addison Emery Verrill.   *American Journal of Science*, 4th series,
     vol. 9, no. 53 (May 1900), p. 313-40.

Based on a course of six lectures delivered by Verrill at the Lowell Institute in Boston in November and December 1899. He discusses the subsidence and re-elevation of Bermuda over time; the nature and origin of the islands' white sands; subaerial and littoral erosion; hurricanes; early maps and sketches; and changes in the climate. Among his conclusions, Verrill states that the present islands are a small remnant of a very much larger island; that over time the land has sunk by 80 to 100 feet; that the white sand and mud consist of small molluscan shells; that erosion has occurred on a grand scale but the rate of erosion by the sea has been greatly exaggerated by most writers; that the islands' red soil and other native soils are the residue left after the destruction and solution of limestones; and that over time the islands' climate has cooled.

74   **Changes of level in the Bermuda Islands.**
     Ralph S. Tarr.   *American Geologist*, vol. 19, no. 5 (May 1897),
     p. 293-303.

Tarr studied the development of Bermuda as revealed by its topography and stratigraphy during a two-week field trip in March 1896. He concludes that the base rock of the island was formed by waves which ground up shell fragments upon the beach. This shell sand beach was then consolidated into dense limestone which was eventually eroded by air and attacked by waves.

75   **Notes on the geology of the Bermudas.**
     John J. Stevenson.   *Transactions of the New York Academy of
     Sciences*, vol. 16 (18 Jan. 1897), p. 96-124.

An early, detailed examination of the geology of Bermuda. After providing a general introduction to the island, Stevenson discusses a variety of rock deposits (clay, dune sands, calcium carbonates, beach deposits and limestone), the island's topography, reefs and lagoons, Harrington Sound, Castle Harbour and the Boundary reef along Bermuda's south shore. He has also included the observations of several knowledge-able geologists, and ends his article with extensive conclusions and analyses regarding Bermuda's geological history.

76   **A visit to the Bermudas in March, 1894.**
     Alexander Agassiz.   *Bulletin of the Museum of Comparative Zoology*,
     vol. 26, no. 2 (April 1895), p. 209-81.

In this early account, Agassiz provides information on eolian hills and dunes, fossils, sounds and lagoons, the distribution of corals, ledge flats and patches, serpuline reefs and pot-holes. Agassiz's early investigations are an excellent basis for further study. There are thirty black-and-white plates following p. 281 on unnumbered pages.

77   **On the geology of the Bermudas.**
     Richard J. Nelson.   *Transactions of the Geological Society of London*,
     2nd series, vol. 5, pt. 1 (1837), p. 103-23.

This is among the earliest investigations of the geology of Bermuda. Nelson, stationed on Bermuda with the Royal Navy at different times between 1827 and 1833, gives a general but detailed introduction to the geology of the area. He comments on alluvium; land on sea, sea on land, and sand encroachments; organic formations, especially chalk; reefs; caverns; and water. He also provides geological details for the principal islands, particularly St. George's Island, Bermuda and Ireland Island.

Caves

78 **Bermuda's caves: a non-renewable resource.**
Thomas M. Iliffe. *Environmental Conservation*, vol. 6, no. 3 (Autumn 1979), p. 181-86.
Bermuda has one of the highest concentrations of caves known in the world. Iliffe examines in detail the history of the caves and analyses the planned strategies for cave conservation. He considers cave speleothems (stalactites, stalagmites and columns; flowstone, rimstone dams and cave pearls; helectites; and clear blue sea-water pools); special flora and fauna (ferns, mosses and cave-adapted animals); the economic, social and scientific importance of caves; and their destruction. Iliffe concludes with recommendations for conserving this non-renewable resource.

79 **An introduction to the caves of Bermuda.**
Russel S. Harmon. *The Canadian Caver*, no. 6 (1974), p. 52-57.
This brief description of the caves and karst areas of Bermuda is based on a week-long field trip in May 1973. Harmon visited seventeen caves but provides information on all fifty-three caves found in Bermuda. Most of his information is presented in list form. He names each cave as well as giving its location, the status of the cave (open, closed, gated, flooded, destroyed) and his source for the information. He also provides a table of speleothem analyses.

80 **Origin of Bermuda caves.**
J. Harlen Bretz. *National Speleological Society Bulletin*, vol. 22, no. 1 (Jan. 1960), p. 19-22.
Bretz explains that Bermuda caves were originally formed by rainwater and groundwater, and were affected by the rise of the sea level. They now contain salt water pools at tide level but fresh groundwater no longer exists. This short piece also contains a brief discussion of the paper by other scientists.

81 **The caves of Bermuda.**
A. C. Swinnerton. *Geological Magazine*, vol. 66, no. 2 (Feb. 1929), p. 79-84.
A brief introduction to the general geology of Bermuda precedes a more detailed discussion of the island's caves. Swinnerton provides information on the rate of stalactite growth, constructional and destructional depressions, the relation of the sea level and the water table to the formation of the caves, and the dates and history of cave formation.

Hydrogeology

82 **Bermuda.**
Mark P. Rowe. In: *Hydrology and water resources of small islands: a practical guide.* Edited by A. Falkland. Paris: Unesco, 1991, p. 333-38. (Studies and Reports in Hydrology, no. 49).
This volume was prepared to assist technicians, hydrologists, engineers and managers in the identification, assessment, development, management and protection of water resources. The section on Bermuda (case-study no. 3) outlines the island's groundwater resources. Rowe discusses Bermuda's groundwater policies and development strategies concerning groundwater management and exploitation.

83 **The freshwater 'Central Lens' of Bermuda.**
Mark P. Rowe. *Journal of Hydrology,* vol. 73, no. 1/2 (1984), p. 165-76.
Rowe presents the results of an eight-year study (1975-82) of Bermuda's central groundwater lens bounded by the less permeable limestone Paget Formation and the more permeable limestone Belmont Formation. He provides useful information for determining groundwater resources.

84 **Hydrogeology of Bermuda: significance of an across-the-island variation in permeability.**
H. Leonard Vacher. *Journal of Hydrology,* vol. 39 (1978), p. 207-26.
Vacher concludes that the distribution of fresh groundwater is a reflection of the forces exerted by the low permeable limestones of the Paget Formation and the older, more highly permeable limestones of the Belmont Formation. The Paget Formation acts as a dam for the groundwater lens while the Belmont Formation acts as a drain.

85 **Hydrogeochemistry of Bermuda: a case history of ground-water diagenesis of biocalcarenites.**
L. N. Pummer, H. Leonard Vacher, Fred T. Mackenzie, O. P. Bricker, Lynton S. Land. *Geological Society of America Bulletin,* vol. 87 (Sept. 1976), p. 1,301-16.
The authors have examined in detail the hydrochemistry of the Bermuda phreatic zone to clarify the chemical processes that produce the observed and documented phreatic diagenesis. Examination of the groundwater chemistry enabled the authors to map the extent of mixing of meteoric groundwater and sea water; the extent of saturation with calcite and aragonite; the concentration of strontium; and the amount of calcium and magnesium derived from the limestone. They found that three processes control the chemistry of Bermudian groundwater: the generation of elevated carbon dioxide pressures in the soils and marshes; the dissolution of carbonate minerals, principally aragonite; and the mix with sea water.

Reefs

86 **Holocene reefs of Bermuda.**
Alan Logan. Miami Beach, Florida: University of Miami,
Comparative Sedimentary Laboratory, 1988. 62p. 6 maps. bibliog.
(Sedimenta XI).

In this guidebook to the reefs, Logan describes aspects of both their geology and
biology. He divides the reefs into three major types: platform margin reefs; lagoonal
reefs; and inshore reefs. He also provides a comparison of Bermuda reefs and
Caribbean and West Indian reefs, and discusses the biotic factors affecting Bermudian
reefs. Finally, there is a comprehensive review of previous studies in this area
beginning as early as 1837.

87 **Holocene reefs and sediments of Castle Harbour, Bermuda.**
Stephen Dryer, Alan Logan. *Journal of Marine Research*, vol. 36,
no. 3 (1978), p. 399-425.

Dryer and Logan's study has three objectives: to determine the abundance, diversity,
geographical and bathymetric distribution of main reef-building coral species on
fringing and patch reefs; to determine textual and compositional trends which might
exist for the sediments of the harbour; and to determine the effect of dredging on
corals and sediments. The authors discuss three reef types found in Bermuda and
describe five major habitats for coral colonization.

88 **Bermuda's reef-front platform: bathymetry and significance.**
Daniel J. Stanley, Donald J. P. Swift. *Marine Geology*, vol. 6 (1968),
p. 479-500.

Stanley and Swift have examined the outer reef and the reef-front platform that
surround Bermuda. The submerged platform extends to over three nautical miles
seaward of an elliptical reef tract. They describe the physiology of this structure and
show its relation to recent geological events. The authors conclude that the reef tract
and the submerged platform are a result of physical rather than biological processes.
The reef-front platform is erosional in nature and is related to processes effective
during the Quaternary period.

89 **Bermuda's southern aeolianite reef tract.**
Daniel J. Stanley, Donald J. P. Swift. *Science*, vol. 157 (11 Aug.
1967), p. 677-81.

The authors investigated southeastern reef formations to determine whether they were
formed by coral growth or from consolidations of windblown sand. They concluded
that the formations were submerged dune ridges covered with a thin veneer of
encrusting organisms – eolianites deposited on an old truncated surface known as a
reef-front terrace.

Travel Guides

90 **Bermuda.**
   Glenda Bendure, Ned Friary.   Hawthorn, Australia: Lonely Planet
   Publications, 1997. 171p. 19 maps. (Lonely Planet Travel Survival Kit).
Travel guides in the Lonely Planet series emphasize travel for independent people and show a concern for a country's culture, natural resources and features, and wildlife. This guide provides general information about Bermuda and travel suggestions for the visitor; information on transport and outdoor activities; and sections on Hamilton and the individual parishes.

91 **Adventure guide to Bermuda.**
   Blair Howard.   Edison, New Jersey: Hunter Publishing, 1996. 159p.
   8 maps.
Emphasizes outdoor activities including diving, fishing, golfing and other sports. There is also practical information concerning dining and accommodation. Ferry and bus schedules are an added feature.

92 **Bermuda guide: your passport to great travel!**
   Ron Charles.   Washington, DC: Open Road Publishing, 1995. 242p.
   4 maps.
This very detailed guide is written in a friendly and casual style. General information on sports and recreation, and shopping is followed by separate chapters for each of the nine Bermudian parishes. In each of these chapters, there are very good descriptions of available accommodation and restaurants, as well as detailed tours. A separate section on the 'Best of Bermuda' highlights accommodation and restaurants.

93 **Insight pocket guides Bermuda.**
David F. Raine.   Singapore: Hofer Communications, 1994. 90p.
7 maps. bibliog.

Provides a quick and practical reference for travellers who wish to make the best use of a short stay. Contents include information on history and culture, shopping, dining and nightlife, and accommodation. Raine also includes suggested itineraries and excursions, a calendar of annual events and a large fold-out map.

94 **Frommer's Bermuda.**
Darwin Porter, Danforth Price.   New York: Macmillan Travel, 1993- .
annual. (Frommer's Complete Travel Guides).

Provides information on accommodation, dining, sightseeing and walking tours, sports and recreation, shopping and nightlife. There is also a separate section listing the 'Best of Bermuda': beaches and dive sites, outdoor activities, views, resorts and restaurants. This publication began as *Frommer's dollarwise guide to Bermuda and the Bahamas* in 1986. In 1990 it was renamed *Frommer's Bermuda and the Bahamas, plus Turks and Caicos* and in the following year became *Frommer's comprehensive travel guide, Bermuda and the Bahamas*. Bermuda received its own separate guide in 1993.

95 **Bermuda.**
Ken Berstein.   Oxford: Berlitz Publishing Co., 1992. 9th ed. 128p.
3 maps. (Berlitz Pocket Guides).

This guide provides an overview and brief history of Bermuda, information on what to see and do, and what kinds of food to eat. Unlike similar publications, it does not list or recommend restaurants or accommodation. Its small size makes it convenient to carry, but for planning purposes, it should be used in conjunction with a more detailed guide.

96 **Bermuda shipwrecks.**
Daniel Berg, Denise Berg.   East Rockway, New York: Aqua Explorers,
1991. 72p. map.

This is a diver's, tourist's and historian's guide to fifty-six shipwrecks in the waters around Bermuda. For each shipwreck, the authors provide a history of the wreck and a description of the dive site. Black-and-white and colour photographs accompany the text. Also included are colour illustrations of the postage stamps which commemorate seventeen of the wrecks.

97 **Birnbaum's Bermuda.**
Edited by Alexandra Mayes Birnbaum.   New York: Harper Perennials,
1991- . annual. (A Stephen Birnbaum Travel Guide).

This guide is divided into five major sections: 'Getting Ready To Go' (with guidelines on travelling to Bermuda, insurance, currency, communications, consular services and customs regulations); 'The Island' (with information on museums and galleries, shopping, sports and fitness, nightlife and the best accommodation and restaurants); 'Diversions' (historic homes and gardens, forts and diving); 'Directions' (a variety of walking tours); and 'Glossary'. A very handy and portable guide, it continues, in part, *Birnbaum's Caribbean, Bermuda, and the Bahamas*.

98   Diving Bermuda.

Jesse Cancelmo, Mike Stropher.   New York: Aqua Quest Publications, 1990. 128p. map.

The authors provide information on accommodation, shopping, dining, dive shops and dive safety. There are also descriptions of twenty shipwrecks which give the name of the wreck, its depth, when it was sunk, the type of craft and its length. Finally, the authors describe one reef site and nine snorkelling sites. The book is heavily illustrated with colour plates.

99   The islands of Bermuda: another world.

David F. Raine.   London: Macmillan, 1990. 130p. 4 maps.

This unusual travel guide provides a wealth of information for visitors to Bermuda but does not describe or recommend accommodation and restaurants. Raine does cover history, government, flora and fauna, architecture, the Bermuda Triangle, Bermudian traditions, food, medicinal folklore, the arts, nightlife and sightseeing, conservation and sports. Appendices give information about government ministries, art galleries and churches. Sixty-five colour photographs are scattered throughout the text.

100   Yachting guide to Bermuda.

Jane Harris, Edward Harris.   Mangrove Bay, Bermuda: Bermuda Maritime Museum Press; Fort Lauderdale, Florida: Bluewater Books & Charts, 1988. 144p. 17 maps.

This comprehensive guide to the waters of Bermuda provides detailed descriptions of the approaches to the island and the anchorages that are available. The authors caution, however, that the guide is simple and that the official charts should be used for all navigation. The work was first published in 1977 as *Yachtsman's guide to the Bermuda Islands* by Michael Voegeli.

101   Christmas in Bermuda.

Nan Lyons, Ivan Lyons.   *Bon Appetit*, vol. 32, no. 2 (Dec. 1987), p. 48, 50, 52, 54, 194.

The authors describe Christmas celebrations in Bermuda and provide information on accommodation and restaurants. There are recipes for a traditional Bermuda breakfast (codfish, potatoes and bananas), fish chowder and lamb chops Tante Lucie. Lyrics for a Bermudian version of 'The Twelve Days of Christmas' are also included.

102   Bermuda.

Ben Carruthers, edited by R. C. Fisher.   New York: Fisher Travel Guides, 1983- . annual. (Fisher's World Travel Guides).

This guide begins with a detailed introduction to the island and presents a great many facts which are of use to the tourist, as well as background information on the history, the people, and the food and drink. There are separate sections for Hamilton, St. George's and the individual parishes. The guide highlights dining and accommodation, shopping, sightseeing, sports and churches although no addresses or telephone numbers are given for most of the hotels and restaurants.

103   **Fielding's Bermuda and the Bahamas.**
Rachel J. Christmas, Walter Christmas.   Redondo Beach, California:
Fielding Worldwide, 1983- . annual. (Fielding Travel Guides).

Provides information on when to go to Bermuda and how to get there, as well as on sports, sightseeing, dining, the economy, nightlife, shopping and accommodation. Hotels, restaurants and some tourist sights are rated with stars and prices are given. Most of the information is divided according to parishes.

104   **Fodor's Bermuda.**
New York: Fodor's Travel Publications, 1980- . annual. (Fodor's
Modern Guide).

This very useful and comprehensive guide provides a great deal of practical information concerning accommodation, dining, sports and recreation, the arts and nightlife, and shopping. The annual guide began publication in 1960 under the title *Fodor's guide to the Caribbean, Bahamas, and Bermuda.* The publication subsequently became *Fodor's Caribbean, Bahamas, and Bermuda* and then in 1980, *Fodor's Bermuda.*

Travel Accounts

105 Holiday in Bermuda 1889: a photo essay.

Donald E. Stephens. Lunenburg, Vermont: Stinehour Press, 1993.
107p. bibliog.

Jacob V. B. Prince was one of the first tourists to record his vacation on film. Stephens combines Prince's photographs and contemporary textual sources to produce a travel account of Prince's trip to Bermuda in February 1889. His seventy-nine photographs have been reproduced in their original size of 3″ × 4″ which means that some details are lost due to the small size. Bermudian archivist, John Adams, has added an 'Historical Addendum' with comments on each of the photographs.

106 Bermuda as it used to be.

David F. Raine. St. George, Bermuda: Pompano Publications, 1986.
122p.

Like Jacob V. B. Prince (see preceding item), Edith Ross Parker was one of the first visitors to record her Bermuda trip on film. This volume includes eighty-two black-and-white photographs from her March/April 1899 visit. In this unique travel account and historical record, Raine complements her pictures of scenic views, people and buildings with a text that attempts to 'reconstruct Edith Parker's complete visit so we can wander around with her' (p. 7). Raine has published a similar book, *Through distant eyes* (St. George, Bermuda: Pompano Publications, 1997), using the account of six individuals who visited Bermuda between 1859 and 1883.

107 Here, there and everywhere.

Frederic Hamilton. London: Hodder & Stoughton; New York:
George H. Doran, 1921. 6th ed. 304p.

In Lord Hamilton's record of his travels to India and the Far East, the West Indies, South America and France, his sojourn in Bermuda appears in chapter seven (p. 169-96). There is no precise indication when Hamilton visited but it appears to be after the First World War. He comments on history, vegetation, climate, fishing, government, architecture and society. This book also appears in *My yesterdays* (Garden City, New York: Doubleday, Doran, 1930) along with Hamilton's *The vanished pomps of yesterday* and *The days before yesterday*.

108 A Bermudan sojourn.

William Dean Howells. *Harpers Monthly Magazine*, vol. 124, no. 739 (Dec. 1911), p. 16-27.

This travel account offers gentle comments on the beauty of the island, its history, the people and their religions, architecture, flora and fauna, and Hamilton and St. George's. Six colour reproductions of paintings by Norman J. Black appear in the text and a full-page colour plate is inserted between p. 16 and p. 17.

109 Ten thousand miles on a bicycle.

Karl Kron. New York: Published by the Author, 1887. Reprinted, New York: E. Rosenblatt, 1982. 799p.

An account of the author's world-wide cycling trip made between May 1879 and April 1884. His experiences on Bermuda, where he cycled a total of 142 miles, are related in chapter twenty-five, 'The coral reefs of Bermuda' (p. 353-70). Quoting extensively from a number of sources, Kron (a pseudonym for Lyman Hotchkiss Bagg) comments on flora, geography, topography and the people of the island.

110 Bermuda: an idyl of the Summer Islands.

Julia Caroline Ripley Dorr. New York: Charles Scribner's Sons, 1884. 148p. map.

Describing her visit to Bermuda in March 1883, Dorr comments on the flora, geography, social life and social conditions of both the whites and the blacks. This is an excellent description of late 19th-century life in Bermuda.

111 Stark's illustrated Bermuda guide.

James Henry Stark. Boston, Massachusetts: Photo-Electrotype Co., 1884. 192p. 4 maps.

This combined history and travel guide covers such topics as climate, agriculture, manners and customs, government, education, religion, and geology. The last thirty-five pages contain advertisements for Bermudian hotels, restaurants and businesses. Along with Godet's *Bermuda* (see item no. 114), this is one of the more useful of the 19th-century guides, and contains sixteen photographs and thirteen engravings.

112 Bermudian days.

Julia Caroline Ripley Dorr. *Atlantic Monthly*, vol. 52, no. 314 (Dec. 1883), p. 778-91.

This thoughtful account of the author's trip from New York to Bermuda in March 1883 provides a good description of late 19th-century Bermuda, in particular, the climate and the social conditions. This article formed the basis of her 1884 book (see item no. 110).

113 **Bermuda.**
Christiana Rounds. *Harper's New Monthly Magazine*, vol. 48, no. 286 (March 1874), p. 484-500.

Offering a blend of facts, graphic description and anecdotes, Rounds discusses the government, social conditions, and religion in 19th-century Bermuda. She suggests that her comments constitute just a survey and that '[m]ore critical observations will require six months or a year' (p. 500). Thirteen black-and-white engravings and two maps are included.

114 **Bermuda: its history, geology, climate, products, agriculture, commerce, and government, from the earliest period to the present time; with hints to invalids.**
Theodore L. Godet. London: Smith, Elder, 1860. 271p.

Godet, a Bermudian medical doctor, wrote this book 'to give an historical account of the origin and progress of the settlement made by emigrants from England in Bermuda . . . and of the constitutional establishment, internal government, and political system maintained by Great Britain in these Islands . . . to describe the manners and dispositions of the present inhabitants, as influenced by climate, situation, and other local causes; and [offer] some observations on the character and genius of the coloured race in the colony' (Preface, p. v). Contents include information on history, climate, government, legislation, fisheries, topography, agriculture, population, education, manners and customs, natural history, shells and corals. Appendices list temperatures, exports and imports, as well as a variety of other statistics.

Tourism

115 Importance of tourism for the economy of Bermuda.
Brian Archer. *Annals of Tourism Research*, vol. 22, no. 4 (1995), p. 918-30.

The aim of this paper is to compare the effect of tourism on the economy of Bermuda with the impact made by other economic sectors. Archer concludes that tourism has declined in the last decade but is still the major employer; that international finance and business activity has increased; that the closing of three military bases from 1993 to 1995 will have a distinct economic impact; and that constant monitoring of tourism and the island's image is necessary. The article contains five tables of tourism-related statistics.

116 Statistical Review.
Bermuda. Department of Tourism. Hamilton, Bermuda: The Department, 1989- . annual.

This annual publication consists almost entirely of statistical tables with minimal text or commentary. The tables include figures for air arrivals, hotel statistics, exit survey data and comparisons with Caribbean countries.

117 Tourism in the Bahamas and Bermuda: two case studies.
Brian Archer. Bangor, Wales: University of Wales Press, 1977. 87p. 2 maps. (Bangor Occasional Papers in Economics, no. 10).

The principal objective of this study is to trace the flow of the average tourist dollar through the economies of each of the two countries. In chapter five (p. 58-83), which deals with Bermuda, Archer provides geographical and historical background for the island, information on the present economic situation, a description of recent developments in the tourism industry, and his principal findings and conclusions. Fourteen tables of figures and statistics are included in the chapter.

Flora and Fauna

General

118 **Field guide to the conspicuous flora and fauna of Bermuda.**
A. R. Cavaliere, Robert D. Barnes, C. B. Cook.   Ferry Reach,
Bermuda: Bermuda Biological Station for Research, 1987. 2nd ed. 82p.
bibliog. (Special Publication, no. 28).

Designed to assist with 'rapid identification of common and conspicuous marine life
. . . [and] includes the fringe of land plants encountered above the high tide mark and
in adjacent fields, as well as the most common birds and land animals' (p. 2). The 255
species described include marine algae, sponges, corals and sea anemones, sea worms,
molluscs and crustaceans, sea urchins and sea cucumbers, fishes, plants, reptiles and
birds. There are sixty black-and-white photographs and eighty-five drawings, as well
as a glossary and bibliography. The first edition was published in 1983.

119 **The Bermuda Islands.**
T. A. Stephenson, Anne Stephenson.   *Endeavour*, vol. 13, no. 50
(April 1954), p. 72-80.

A good general introduction to the flora and fauna of Bermuda. The Stephensons
describe and comment on geology, climate, vegetation and marine life. Some interesting comparisons are made with the Florida Keys.

120 **The Bermuda Islands: their scenery, climate, productions,**
physiography, natural history, and geology; with sketches of their
early history and the changes due to man.
Addison Emery Verrill. New Haven, Connecticut: Connecticut
Academy of Arts and Sciences, 1901-02. 544p. map. bibliog.
(*Transactions of the Connecticut Academy of Arts and Sciences*,
vol. 11, part II, p. 413-956).

In this early major treatise, Verrill aims 'to provide a work that may meet most of the
needs of large numbers of persons who go to the islands annually for health, pleasure,
or study, and who may wish to learn as much as possible about the islands and their
principal productions, without being obliged to consult a library, or burden themselves
with many books' (p. 413). The text is divided into three sections: a general description; the island's physiography; and the major section, covering changes in the flora
and fauna due to the intervention of humans. The text contains 245 figures and there
are 39 pages of black-and-white plates between p. 912 and p. 913. There is also an
extensive bibliography.

121 **The Bermuda Islands: a contribution to the physical history and**
zoology of the Somers Archipelago.
Angelo Heilprin. Philadelphia: Published by the Author, 1889. 247p.
bibliog.

Contains a variety of observations and commentary based on the time Heilprin spent in
Bermuda in the summer of 1888. He provides information on coral reefs, geology and a
large section (p. 97-201) on the zoology of Bermuda. He describes a wide range of
species including corals, starfish, crayfish, earwigs, cockroaches, horse flies, spiders and
cuttle fish. The descriptions can range from one word to several paragraphs. There is an
annotated bibliography of literature on coral reefs (p. 202-31), and a section of black-
and-white plates on unnumbered pages following the text. While Heilprin is listed as the
author, there are also contributions from J. Playfair McMurrich (actinology – the science
of the chemical action of light), H. A. Pilsbry (helicoid land molluscs), George Marx
(spiders), P. R. Uhler (insects), and Charles H. Bollman (centipedes and millipedes).

122 **Contributions to the natural history of the Bermuda Islands.**
Angelo Heilprin. *Proceedings of the Academy of Natural Sciences of*
Philadelphia, vol. 40 (1888), p. 302-28.

This article, based on observations made in the summer of 1888, provides a list of
species, with minimal or no annotations, for Actinozoa (thirty species), Echinodermata
(twenty species), and Crustacea (twenty-seven species). Heilprin also describes four
new species of Mollusca.

123 **The naturalist in Bermuda; a sketch of the geology, zoology and**
botany, of that remarkable group of islands; together with
meteorological observations.
John Matthew Jones. London: Reeves & Turner, 1859. 200p. map.

This is among the first comprehensive scientific natural histories of Bermuda.
Although there are sections on geology (p. 1-10) and botany (p. 131-43), the bulk of
the book (p. 11-130) is devoted to the zoology of Bermuda. Jones provides information

31

on the island's mammals, reptiles, fish, molluscs, insects and crustaceans. The information concerning birds is divided into two sections written by Major J. W. Wedderburn and J. L. Hurdis. The section of meteorological observations contains sixteen tables of wind, temperature and precipitation measurements.

124 **Notes on the Bermudas and their natural history, with special reference to their marine algae.**
Alex F. Kemp. *Canadian Naturalist and Geologist*, vol. 2, no. 2 (May 1857), p. 145-56.

In this early account of Bermuda, Kemp discusses the island's geology, climate, flora and fauna, and marine life.

Vegetation

125 **Bermuda: gardens and houses.**
Ian Macdonald-Smith, Sylvia Shorto. New York: Rizzoli, 1996. 204p.

This lush and luxurious book includes 159 captioned colour plates and eight black-and-white photographs by Macdonald-Smith. He has been able to capture the beauty and variety of Bermuda's gardens and the houses they surround. Shorto's text (p. 6-45) is a good complement to the photographs.

126 **Bermuda's botanical wonderland: a field guide.**
Christine Phillips-Watlington. London: Macmillan Education, 1996. 128p. map.

This collection of sketches and watercolours, plus text, is not intended as a comprehensive botanical treatise. Instead, the author's purpose is to 'capture the essence of Bermuda as revealed in its flora' (p. 5) and this has been accomplished with great skill and accuracy. The book includes virtually all of Bermuda's flora and can be used quite handily in the field. The work is considered to be the most comprehensive record since Britton's 1918 *Flora of Bermuda* (see item no. 141).

127 **Human impact on the forests of Bermuda: the decline of endemic cedar and palmetto since 1609, recorded in the Holocene pollen record of Devonshire Marsh.**
Bruce F. Rueger, Theodore N. von Wallmenich. *Journal of Paleolimnology*, vol. 16, no. 1 (July 1996), p. 59-66.

Cedar was used in Bermuda for housing, furniture and small craft construction while the palmetto was used for roof thatching, basketry, woven hats, food and an alcoholic beverage called bibby. Both of these plants have played important roles in Bermuda's history. Using a nine-metre core sample from the Devonshire Marsh, the authors have been able to corroborate the historical record from 1609 to the present. The pollen record in the core matches the impact humans have had on these two examples of endemic flora.

128   Fruits and vegetables of the Caribbean.

M. J. Bourne, G. W. Lennox, S. A. Seddon.   London: Macmillan
Caribbean, 1988. 58p.

This handy, illustrated guide identifies forty-eight of the most commonly found fruits
and vegetables of the region. The authors have described each species' origin, its
botanical characteristics and its uses.

129   Bermuda: her plants and gardens, 1609-1850.

Jill Collett.   London: Macmillan, 1987. 104p. map. bibliog.

This fascinating history of farming, gardens and plants in Bermuda outlines how
Bermuda's social history has affected the farming and gardening of the time. The
work also contains a dictionary of plants in Bermuda; a chronology listing the dates
when various plants were imported into Bermuda; and thirty-two colour plates. This
work has been produced in conjunction with the Bermuda National Trust.

130   Trees of the Caribbean.

S. A. Seddon, G. W. Lennox.   London: Macmillan Caribbean, 1980.
74p.

This guide has been designed as a companion to *Flowers of the Caribbean* (see item
no. 131) and is intended for individuals with little or no botanical training. The trees
are divided into four sections: ornamental trees; fruit trees; coast trees; and palm and
palm-like trees. For each entry, the authors have provided at least one colour
photograph, information regarding leaf shape, size and colour, and descriptions of the
flower and fruit. Each entry also includes the botanical family name and the scientific
and common names.

131   Flowers of the Caribbean.

G. W. Lennox, S. A. Seddon.   London: Macmillan Caribbean, 1978.
72p.

Designed for individuals with little or no botanical training. The flora are divided into
three sections: herbs and shrubs, trees, and orchids. For each of the fifty entries, the
authors have provided a colour photograph, the common, local and scientific names,
and a short description of each specimen. Although this handy guide does not
illustrate all species of flowering plants, it does discuss the more common ones.

132   The Bermuda jubilee garden.

Edited by Elfrida L. Wardman.   Hamilton, Bermuda: The Garden
Club of Bermuda, 1971. 349p.

Written by professional horticulturists and experienced amateur gardeners, this
detailed work describes the types of plants found in a Bermuda garden. For each type
of plant (trees, shrubs, vines, roses) or garden (rock, container, lawns) discussed there
is an introduction and list of plant species. There are also articles on planning a
Bermuda garden; Bermuda soils and plant nutrition; native plants; fruit culture; and
pest and disease control. This work marks the fiftieth anniversary of The Garden Club
of Bermuda and is a revised edition of the Club's 1955 publication, *The Bermuda
garden*.

133 **The struggle for survival of the Bermuda cedar.**
David Challinor, David B. Wingate. *Biological Conservation*, vol. 3, no. 3 (April 1971), p. 220-22.

Examines the origins of the Bermuda cedar and describes the infestation of scale insects that devastated the cedar forests in the 1940s. The authors also outline the attempts at biological control which were undertaken and the natural regeneration which occurred. Finally, they speculate on the future of the cedar population of Bermuda. Five black-and-white photographs accompany the article.

134 **Bermuda: trees and plants: a short guide.**
Kitty Zuill, William Edward Sears Zuill. Hamilton, Bermuda: Bermuda Book Stores, 1955. 3rd ed. 80p.

The Zuills describe twenty-one species of trees, twelve species of shrubs and small trees, and fifteen species of ferns. For each species they give the common and scientific names and a non-scientific prose description. There are nineteen fair quality black-and-white photographs by Walter Rutherford and Frederick L. Hamilton, and four paintings by May Middleton.

135 **The pests of juniper in Bermuda.**
John McLaren Waterston. *Tropical Agriculture*, vol. 26 (1949), p. 5-15.

Waterston begins with a description of the Bermuda cedar, Juniperus bermudiana, and discusses the historical use of cedar in Bermuda. Despite its importance, the cedar was neglected in terms of sylviculture and in the mid-20th century fell prey to scale insects which devastated the cedar population. Waterston gives a chronological outline of the pest problem from 1930 onwards and discusses pest control measures.

136 **The fungi of Bermuda.**
John McLaren Waterston. Hamilton, Bermuda: Bermuda Press, 1947. 305p. 2 maps. bibliog. (Department of Agriculture. Bulletin no. 23).

Brings together various records of fungus collections from Bermuda gathered in the seventy years prior to this report. Waterston provides a good introduction and, in a discussion of previous work in the field, indicates that although there are some early mentions of fungus from the 17th century, major research work in the area did not begin until 1844. A statistical summary (p. 49-60) of the 754 species Waterston has identified precedes the bulk of this work (p. 64-246) which consists of a list of the species. For each entry he gives the species name, the host or substrate where it is found, the location of the collecting station, the date the find was made, and the name of the collector. There is an index of fungi and an index of hosts or substrates. The work contains thirty-eight illustrations and thirteen tables.

137 **The woodlands of Bermuda.**
J. S. Beard. *The Empire Forestry Journal*, vol. 19, no. 2 (1940), p. 258-63.

This article begins with a general account of Bermuda, its climate, topography, soil and other environmental factors. This is followed by a short outline of the island's tree flora and plant communities. Finally, Beard comments on the character and utilization of the Bermuda cedar. This article was written prior to the scale insect infestation which almost destroyed the whole cedar population.

138 **Notes on the flora of the Bermudas.**
A. B. Rendle. *Journal of Botany*, vol. 74 (1936), p. 42-50, 65-71, 101-12.

Basing his article on a ten-week stay from March to May 1933, Rendle gives an overview of contemporary vegetation in this three-part description of Bermudian flora. Although general in nature, the article is accompanied by more scholarly contributions: 'Mosses' by H. N. Dixon (p. 101-02); 'Hepatics' by W. E. Nicholson (p. 102-03); 'Fungi' by F. L. Stephens (p. 103-05); 'Lichens' by A. Lorraine Smith and I. M. Lamb (p. 106); and 'Marine algae' by Geoffrey Tandy (p. 107-10).

139 **Bermuda's 'oldest inhabitants': tales of plant life.**
Louisa Hutchings Smith. Sevenoaks, England: J. Salmon, 1934. 70p.

Smith's 'informal historical sketch of trees and plants in Bermuda' (Preface, p. 5) looks at a wide variety of vegetation including trees, fruits and vegetables. She chronicles accounts of vegetation from the 16th century and gives information on planting from the 17th century. There are also sections on the cedar and palmetto trees, as well as endemic plants. This work would have been more accessible had it included an index.

140 **The cedars of Nonsuch.**
William Beebe. *Atlantic Monthly*, vol. 145 (May 1930), p. 594-600.

In this article, Beebe describes the vegetation of Nonsuch Island, particularly the native cedar trees. Nonsuch Island, situated on the southeast rim of Castle Harbour, was used as a base by Beebe for his extensive underwater explorations off the coast of Bermuda.

141 **Flora of Bermuda.**
Nathaniel Lord Britton. New York: Charles Scribner's Sons, 1918.
Reprinted, New York: Hafner Publishing Co., 1965. 585p. bibliog.

Britton describes and illustrates 519 species from four phyla: Spermatophyta (seed-bearing plants); Pteridophyta (ferns); Bryophyta (mosses); and Thallophyta (algae, fungi and lichens). In his introduction he comments on the variety of flora found in Bermuda and pays particular attention to soil and climate. The work also includes a bibliography, a glossary and an account of twenty-five botanical collections made in Bermuda.

142 **Bermuda fungi.**
Fred J. Seaver. *Memoirs of the New York Botanical Garden*, vol. 6 (1916), p. 501-11.

Seaver's observations were made during a two-week collecting trip in November/December 1912. The list, which Seaver provides, contains 122 specimens of the 'species collected, so far as they have been named' (p. 505). There are four new species listed: Ascophanus bermudensis, Nectria lantanae, Calonectria umbelliferarum and Calonectria granulosa. In the text which accompanies this list of fungi, Seaver describes generally the species which were collected.

143 **The lichens of Bermuda.**
Lincoln W. Riddle. *Bulletin of the Torrey Botanical Club*, vol. 43,
no. 3 (March 1916), p. 145-60.

Together with a list of eighty-six species, Riddle outlines previous reports and collections. Seven new species are described in detail; otherwise descriptions of species are limited.

144 **Mosses of Bermuda.**
Elizabeth G. Britton. *Bulletin of the Torrey Botanical Club*, vol. 42,
no. 2 (Feb. 1915), p. 71-76.

Britton points out that her own and previous studies indicate that Bermuda is not rich in mosses. This article provides a list of twenty-eight species. There is little or no description given for the species listed.

145 **Gardens of Bermuda.**
Nathaniel Lord Britton. *Journal of the New York Botanical Garden*,
vol. 14 (1913), p. 172-76.

In this short article Britton describes four public gardens (the public gardens in Hamilton and St. George's, the Par-la-Ville garden in Hamilton, and the gardens of the Agricultural Station in Paget) and the variety of flowering plants and trees found in them. Britton visited Bermuda in August and September 1912.

146 **Botanical exploration in Bermuda.**
Nathaniel Lord Britton. *Journal of the New York Botanical Garden*,
vol. 13 (1912), p. 189-94.

The material presented here was gathered by Britton on two trips to Bermuda in 1912, 26 August to 21 September, and 29 November to 14 December. Britton lists seventeen endemic flowering plants, ferns and mosses with an additional list of four species thought to be endemic. He rejects the idea that Bermuda ever had land connections and suggests three methods by which flora species were transported to Bermuda: sea-borne seeds; wind-borne seeds; and seeds transported by birds. The article includes five black-and-white plates: plate 103 precedes p. 189; plates 104 and 105 are placed between p. 190 and p. 191; plate 106 comes between p. 192 and p. 193; and plate 107 follows p. 194.

147 **Notes on the flora of the Bermudas.**
Stewardson Brown. *Proceedings of the Academy of Natural Sciences
of Philadelphia*, vol. 61 (Nov. 1910), p. 486-94.

During three visits to Bermuda in 1905, 1908 and 1909, Brown collected over 700 species of flora; however, this paper considers only endemic species among the flowering plants. He lists and briefly describes fifty-nine species. Of these, two are new species and described in detail: Peperomia septentrionalis and Chiococca bermudiana. Brown precedes his species list with a general introduction to the flora habitats, a discussion of species introduced by man, and a commentary on the spread of flora throughout the islands.

148   **The plant formations of the Bermuda Islands.**
       John W. Harshberger. *Proceedings of the Academy of Natural
       Sciences of Philadelphia*, vol. 57 (Oct. 1905), p. 695-700.
Based on observations conducted in June 1905, Harshberger describes nine
formations: marine algal, mangrove swamp, salt marsh, brackish marsh, sand dune,
cliff rock, cedar forest, limestone sinks forest and scrub. For each formation he lists
the species found but provides no descriptions.

149   **Report on the botany of the Bermudas and various other islands of
       the Atlantic and southern oceans: First part.**
       William Botting Hemsley. In: *Report on the scientific results of the
       voyage of H. M. S. Challenger during the years 1873-76. Botany*.
       Vol. I. Article II.   Edited by John Murray.   Edinburgh, London:
       Printed for HMSO by Ballantyne, Hanson and Co., 1885. Reprinted,
       New York: Johnson Reprint, 1965, p. 1-161.
In the introductory notes (p. 1-15) Hemsley discusses the physical condition of the
Bermudas, the island's climate and the vegetation. The bulk of the study (p. 16-128) is
an enumeration of the 524 plant species (plus an addendum list of 9 species) which
were gathered during the voyage. The index (p. 129-35) is followed by thirteen plates
on unnumbered pages. The botanical collections were gathered by H. N. Moseley
during the cruise and dispatched directly to the Royal Gardens at Kew where Hemsley
conducted his work.

150   **On the vegetation of the Bermudas.**
       John Matthew Jones. *Proceedings and Transactions of the Nova
       Scotian Institute of Natural Sciences*, vol. 3 (1873), p. 237-80.
In the text, Jones gives a description of Bermuda's geology in order to show its effect
on vegetation. He also provides some comments on climate and discusses the origins
of plant life on the islands. Most of the article consists of a list of 116 species with
brief descriptions for some.

Marine life

General

151   **Exploring Bermuda's underwater mountainside: a ROM
       expedition studies life in the unknown regions of the ocean floor.**
       Dale R. Calder. *Rotunda*, vol. 26, no. 2 (Fall 1993), p. 18-27.
Calder describes two dives made by an expedition sponsored by the Royal Ontario
Museum in March 1993. The American submersible, *Alvin*, was used to investigate
and collect hydroids at depths greater than 100 metres. The article describes ocean life
at 3,550 metres, the depth to which members of the expedition dove. A separate
article, entitled 'The story of *Alvin*', appears on p. 27.

152 **Bermuda's marine life.**
Wolfgang Sterrer. Hamilton, Bermuda: Bermuda Natural History
Museum and Bermuda Zoological Society, 1992. 307p.

This affordable and readable guide to 225 of the most commonly encountered marine
organisms found in the waters off Bermuda provides descriptions accompanied by 310
illustrations, 60 of which are in colour. Contents include bacteria and algae; plants;
sponges; sea anemones, corals and jellyfish; sea worms; sea spiders, shrimps and
lobsters; molluscs; sea mosses; starfish, sea urchins and sea cucumbers; and fish, eels
and rays. Sterrer also includes twenty-eight useful concept boxes which contain the
author's asides.

153 **A guide to the ecology of shoreline and shallow-water marine
communities of Bermuda.**
Martin L. H. Thomas, Alan Logan. Ferry Reach, Bermuda: Bermuda
Biological Station for Research, 1992. 345p. 19 maps. bibliog. (Special
Publication, no. 30).

After providing a general introduction to the climate, oceanography and human
ecology of Bermuda, the authors examine in detail the individual marine communities
they are studying. For each environment, Thomas and Logan give a description of the
physical and biotic features and conditions, indicate the sites that are most accessible
for study, and discuss the plants and animals that will be encountered. This work
includes eighteen tables, a taxonomic or species index and an extensive bibliography.

154 **Wonders of the deep: underwater Bermuda.**
Toronto: Boulton Publishing Services, 1988. 122p. map.

Features the photographs of five of Bermuda's most experienced underwater photo-
graphers: Michael Burke, Stephen Kerr, Alan Marquardt, Robert Power and Russell
Whayman. The 112 colour plates, accompanied by short commentaries, capture the
beauty of Bermudian reefs, shipwrecks, caves and sea creatures. Neither a guide to
dive sites nor a guide to underwater life, it is certainly an excellent pictorial
introduction to Bermuda's marine world. The map shows the locations of the principal
reefs and shipwrecks photographed.

155 **Marine fauna and flora of Bermuda: a systematic guide to the
identification of the marine organisms.**
Edited by Wolfgang Sterrer. New York: Wiley, 1986. 742p. 2 maps.
bibliog.

This detailed and well-illustrated guide for scientists, teachers, students and nature
lovers lists more than 1,500 species representing the majority of species one would
expect to encounter in the coastal and offshore waters of Bermuda. The contributions
come from sixty-seven recognized authorities. There is a useful glossary.

156   **A field guide to coral reefs of the Caribbean and Florida: a guide to the common invertebrates and fishes of Bermuda, the Bahamas, southern Florida, the West Indies, and the Caribbean coast of Central and South America.**
Eugene Herbert Kaplan.   Boston, Massachusetts: Houghton Mifflin, 1982. 289p. map. bibliog. (Peterson Field Guide Series, no. 27).

This book is sponsored by the National Audubon Society and the National Wildlife Federation. Following a very good introductory chapter, Kaplan provides an overview of coral reefs, their development and their ecology. The bulk of the work is devoted to the animals of the lagoon and the reef. As the book is intended for laypeople, technical terms are kept to a minimum and a glossary is provided. Although Kaplan tries to cover too much, and arguably should have dismissed invertebrates or fish, the book does make interesting reading. The work is illustrated by thirty-seven coloured plates. Stokes' *Handguide to the coral reef fishes . . .* (see item no. 170) may be more useful as a field guide because the illustrations are accorded more attention than the text.

157   **The Harrington Sound project, Kiel University.**
G. Wefer, R. Dawson, G. Hempel.   St. Georges West, Bermuda: Bermuda Biological Station, 1981. 94p. (Special Publication, no. 19).

Scientists, students and technicians from Kiel University, Germany, studied the physical, chemical, biological and geological interaction between water columns and the sea bed in the Kiel Bight in the Western Baltic. Their findings were then compared with Harrington Sound because of the similarities in depth and sea bed conditions. This document reports on three field studies conducted in August/September 1977, March/April 1978 and September/October 1978. There are three sections: a collection of three reports and data files; eight extended summaries of publications arising from the research; and fifteen abstracts from recently published literature pertaining to the research.

158   **Seashore life of Florida and the Caribbean: a guide to the common marine invertebrates and plants of the Atlantic from Bermuda and the Bahamas to the West Indies and the Gulf of Mexico.**
Gilbert L. Voss.   Miami, Florida: Banyan, 1980. rev. ed. 199p. map. bibliog.

The species which Voss includes in this guide represent only a small part of the total fauna – those that one might reasonably expect to find down to a depth of fifty feet. Nevertheless, this book includes a great many species from thirteen invertebrate phyla (sponges, jellyfish, corals, sea anemones, sea fans, flatworms, ribbon worms, sea slugs, squids, crustaceans, sea stars, sea urchins and sea cucumbers) and four plant phyla (algae and sea grasses). Each entry is written in a simple, easy-to-read style. There are also 400 drawings, 19 very good colour photographs and a glossary.

159 **Beneath the seas of the West Indies: Caribbean, Bahamas, Bermuda.**
Hans W. Hannau, Bernd H. Mock. New York: Hastings House; Miami, Florida: Argos, 1973. 104p.

Hannau and Mock offer a discussion of reefs and reef ecology, as well as marine archaeology in the West Indies. The book includes 54 large colour plates and 120 small colour plates, plus a picture portfolio for the identification of exotic, tropical fish which inhabit reef areas.

160 **The zooplankton of the upper waters of the Bermuda area of the North Atlantic.**
Hilary B. Moore. *Bulletin of the Bingham Oceanographic Collection*, vol. 12, no. 2 (Jan. 1949), p. 1-97.

This paper, based on studies carried out from 1938 to 1940, surveys the zooplankton of the upper 300 metres of the ocean. Moore describes the collecting methods and collection locations, provides data for each species found, gives a general discussion of the results of the study, and appends an extensive bibliography. Moore's study includes species from six classes: Coelenterata, Chaetognatha, Mollusca, Crustacea, Cephalochorda and Tunicata. The study includes 208 charts and graphs scattered throughout the text.

161 **Half mile down.**
William Beebe. New York: Harcourt, Brace, 1934. 344p. bibliog.

A complete account of Beebe's underwater research off the coast of Bermuda in the early 1930s. Using a revolutionary bathysphere designed by Otis Barton, Beebe made thirty-five dives just off the south shore. Parts of some of the chapters have appeared in *National Geographic Magazine*, *New York Times Magazine*, *Harper's Monthly Magazine*, and *McCall's Magazine*. There are eight appendices, including Appendix G (p. 295-329) which provides descriptions of the organisms observed on Beebe's dives. This work contains 123 black-and-white illustrations and 8 colour plates. *Half mile down* was republished in 1951 (New York: Duell, Sloan and Pearce).

162 **A half mile down.**
William Beebe. *National Geographic Magazine*, vol. 66, no. 6 (Dec. 1934), p. 661-704.

This is a full summation of the bathysphere dives which Beebe made off the coast of Bermuda during 1934. During this season of diving, Beebe achieved a record depth of 3,028 feet. There are twenty-eight black-and-white photographs and one map. Two separate sections, each containing reproductions of eight colour paintings by Else Bostelmann, have been inserted into the article: 'Flashes from ocean depths' (p. 677-84) and 'Carnivores of a lightless world' (p. 693-700). The paintings represent specimens of marine fauna encountered by Beebe during his dives. This article, along with earlier ones, became the basis for a full-length book, *Half mile down* (see preceding item).

163   **The depths of the sea: strange life forms a mile below the surface.**
William Beebe.   *National Geographic Magazine*, vol. 61, no. 1
(Jan. 1932), p. 64-88.
In this follow-up to his June 1931 article (see item no. 165), Beebe continues to report
on his research of the marine fauna off the coast of Bermuda. There are thirteen black-
and-white photographs of specimens collected. A separate section entitled 'Fantastic
sea life from abyssmal depths' (p. 71-78) contains reproductions of eight colour
paintings by Else Bostelmann which depict some of the specimens Beebe found.

164   **Nonsuch: land of water.**
William Beebe.   New York: Brewer, Warren and Putnam, 1932. 259p.
Beebe describes the research on marine life off the coast of Bermuda which he
conducted in his laboratory on Nonsuch Island at the eastern end of the island. Several
chapters were originally published in *Atlantic Monthly*, *Saturday Evening Post*,
Delineator, *Harper's Monthly Magazine*, and *Nature Magazine*.

165   **A round trip to Davy Jones's locker.**
William Beebe.   *National Geographic Magazine*, vol. 59, no. 6 (June
1931), p. 653-78.
Beebe outlines the origins and use of his bathysphere which was first used in dives off
Bermuda in April 1930. He describes the marine fauna found at various depths to a
maximum of a quarter of a mile. There are fourteen black-and-white photographs.
Another separate section, entitled 'Luminous life in the depths of the sea' (p. 667-74),
contains reproductions of eight colour paintings by Else Bostelmann which depict
some of the fauna Beebe encountered.

Fishes

166   **Background and methods used in studies of the biology of fishes of**
the Bermuda Ocean Acre.
Robert H. Gibbs, Jr., Charles Karnella.   In: *Biology of midwater fishes*
of the Bermuda Ocean Acre.   Edited by Robert H. Gibbs, Jr., William
H. Krueger.   Washington, DC: Smithsonian Institution Press, 1987,
p. 1-31. (Smithsonian Contributions to Zoology, no. 452).
Gibbs and Karnella review the physical and biological oceanography of Bermuda and
describe the sampling strategy, the treatment of the samples, and the methods of
analysis used in studying the midwater fishes of Bermuda.

167   **Family Melamphaidae, bigscales.**
Michael J. Keene.   In: *Biology of midwater fishes of the Bermuda*
Ocean Acre.   Edited by Robert H. Gibbs, Jr., William H. Krueger.
Washington, DC: Smithsonian Institution Press, 1987, p. 169-85.
(Smithsonian Contributions to Zoology, no. 452).
Keene discusses the developmental stages, reproductive cycles, seasonal abundance
and vertical distributions for each of fifteen species in four genera. There are detailed

descriptions and tables for the ten rare species, the two uncommon species, the one common species and the two abundant species.

168 **Family Myctophidae, lanternfishes.**
Charles Karnella. In: *Biology of midwater fishes of the Bermuda Ocean Acre.* Edited by Robert H. Gibbs, Jr., William H. Krueger. Washington, DC: Smithsonian Institution Press, 1987, p. 51-168. (Smithsonian Contributions to Zoology, no. 452).

Discusses the developmental stages, reproductive cycles, seasonal abundance, sex ratios and vertical distributions for each of sixty-three species in eighteen genera. There are detailed descriptions and tables for the twenty rare species, the nineteen uncommon species, the thirteen common species, the six abundant species and the five very abundant species.

169 **Family Sternoptychidae, marine hatchetfishes and related species.**
W. Hunting Howell, William H. Krueger. In: *Biology of midwater fishes of the Bermuda Ocean Acre.* Edited by Robert H. Gibbs, Jr., William H. Krueger. Washington, DC: Smithsonian Institution Press, 1987, p. 32-50. (Smithsonian Contributions to Zoology, no. 452).

In this paper, the authors discuss the developmental stages, the reproductive cycles, the seasonal abundance and the vertical distribution for each of seven species in four genera. The species discussed and described are the two abundant species, the one common species, the one uncommon species and the three rare species.

170 **Handguide to the coral reef fishes of the Caribbean and adjacent tropical waters including Florida, Bermuda and the Bahamas.**
F. Joseph Stokes. New York: Lippincott & Crowell, 1980. 160p.

The emphasis in this handguide is on the illustrations, which are paintings of colour photographs. The descriptions in the text are very short, often consisting of only one sentence or several short phrases. The 460 species described are the fish most likely to be seen by the snorkeller and diver. This book, which includes a glossary, is useful for both professionals and amateurs. Stokes' work is not quite as useful as Goodson's *The many-splendored fishes* . . . (see item no. 172) but is a better field guide than Kaplan's *A field guide to coral reefs* . . . (see item no. 156) because of its emphasis on illustrations.

171 **Fishes of the Caribbean reefs, the Bahamas and Bermuda.**
Ian F. Took. London: Macmillan, 1979. 92p. map.

Introduces some of the more common and spectacular fish to be found around the Caribbean and tropical west Atlantic reefs. For each of the eighty-five species covered, the author provides a description, including length; common and scientific names; a discussion of general habits and particular characteristics; and an indication of where the fish might be found. There are also sections on practical fish watching, underwater photography and conservation of the coral reef. The work is illustrated with seventy-two colour plates of fish and seven of coral.

172 **The many-splendored fishes of the Atlantic coast including the fishes of the Gulf of Mexico, Florida, Bermuda, the Bahamas and the Caribbean.**
Gar Goodson. Palos Verdes Estates, California: Marquest Colorguide Books, 1976. 204p. 2 maps. bibliog.

Written 'primarily as a fishwatcher's guide, this book is also aimed at catching the interest of those who have never looked beneath the surface of the sea' (p. ii). For each of the 408 entries, Goodson provides both the common name and the scientific name, a description, the range of distribution and an indication as to whether it is edible. Though not as complete as Kaplan's *A field guide to coral reefs* . . . (see item no. 156), this volume is more useful than Stokes' *Handguide to the coral reef fishes* . . . (see item no. 170) in terms of textual material.

173 **Field book of the shore fishes of Bermuda and the West Indies.**
William Beebe, John Tee-Van. New York: Dover, 1970. 337p. 2 maps. bibliog.

Originally published under the title *Field book of the shore fishes of Bermuda* in 1933 (New York: G. P. Putnam's Sons). In the introduction, the authors discuss Bermuda fish origins and distribution, migration patterns, fish shape and size, physical features and physiology, food habits and reproduction. The list of species contains 335 entries (323 indigenous species and 12 introduced species). For each, there is a description, a comment on distribution and a pen-and-ink illustration.

174 **Notes on a collection of Bermuda deep-sea fishes.**
Marion Grey. *Fieldiana: Zoology*, vol. 37 (1955), p. 265-302.

Grey describes ninety-one species from thirty-two families of deep-sea fishes in descriptions ranging from one sentence to more than a page. The specimens examined were gathered between July and September 1948. Fourteen illustrations accompany the article.

175 **Preliminary list of Bermuda deep-sea fish.**
William Beebe. *Zoologica*, vol. 22, no. 3 (1937), p. 197-208. bibliog.

Beebe presents this list of 220 species from 46 families in chart form with no descriptions given. The chart gives the family and species names, the number range of specimens gathered, the size range in millimetres and the depth range in fathoms.

176 **New Bermuda fish, including six new species and forty-three species hitherto unrecorded from Bermuda.**
William Beebe, John Tee-Van. *Zoologica*, vol. 13, no. 5 (1932), p. 109-20.

Six new species are described in detail including measurements, physical description and colour. The forty-three previously unrecorded species are listed but no descriptions are given.

177 **A contribution to the ichthyology of Bermuda.**
John Treadwell Nichols. *Proceedings of the Biological Society of Washington*, vol. 33 (24 July 1920), p. 59-64.

Nichols discusses seven previously undescribed species of fish. The specimens had been collected by Louis L. Mowbray and sent to the American Museum of Natural History.

178 **Description of new fishes of Bermuda.**
Tarleton H. Bean. *Proceedings of the Biological Society of Washington*, vol. 25 (31 July 1912), p. 121-26.

Describes eight new species obtained from Louis L. Mowbray during a trip to Bermuda in February 1912.

179 **Notes on Bermudian fishes.**
Thomas H. Barbour. *Bulletin of Comparative Zoology*, vol. 46, no. 7 (1905), p. 109-34.

This paper is based on several collections gathered in 1903 and 1904. Barbour describes 103 species including 4 new ones: Siphostoma dendriticum, Holocentrus puncticulatus, Callionymus bermudarum and Antennarius stellifer. He also provides comments on previous collections and reports.

180 **A preliminary catalogue of the reptiles, fishes and leptocardians of the Bermudas, with descriptions of four species of fishes believed to be new.**
George Brown Goode. *American Journal of Science*, 3rd series, vol. 14, no. 82 (Oct. 1877), p. 289-98.

Goode's catalogue list includes five species of reptile, one species of leptocardia (small, fish-like animals that burrow into the sand) and 159 species of fish. There are no descriptions for any of the species in the list except the four new fish species: Julius nitidissima, Belone jonesii, Atherina harringtonensis and Fundukus rhizophorae.

Coral reefs

181 **Bermuda.**
In: *Coral reefs of the world, 1: Atlantic and eastern Pacific.* Edited by Susan M. Wells. Nairobi: United Nations Environment Programme; Gland, Switzerland; Cambridge, England: International Union for Conservation of Nature and Natural Resources, 1988, p. 49-57.

This article contains a general description of Bermuda reef areas, and information on reef resources, disturbances and deficiencies in Bermuda reefs; Bermudian reef legislation and management; and an extensive list of references. There are also descriptions of two reef preserves: the North Shore Coral Reef Preserve and the South Shore Coral Reef Preserve.

182   **Depth limits of Bermudian Scleractinian corals: a submersible survey.**
       H. Fricke, D. Meischner.   *Marine Biology*, vol. 88, no. 2 (1985), p. 175-87.

In this study, conducted in August and September 1983, the authors describe the distribution, species assemblages and spatial patterns of Scleractinian corals along the outer slopes of the Bermuda atoll. They also investigate influences on coral growth in the area. Fricke and Meischner conclude that Bermuda stony corals have a low growth form diversity; that coral shapes become flatter with depth; and that macro-algae growth is the strongest factor controlling coral growth in deep water.

183   **Coral diseases in Bermuda.**
       Peter Garrett, Hugh Ducklow.   *Nature*, vol. 253, no. 5490 (31 Jan. 1975), p. 349-50.

Basing their article on fieldwork conducted in the summer of 1973, the authors report on coral diseases associated with bacterial infection. Their observations suggest that the diseases may be important agents of coral death.

184   **In the coral reefs of the Caribbean, Bahamas, Florida, Bermuda.**
       Hans W. Hannau.   Garden City, New York: Doubleday, 1974. 135p.

A general introduction to coral reefs, accompanied by ninety-four coloured photographs and twelve black-and-white photographs. Each chapter is by a different contributor which makes the quality a little uneven, and oversimplified material is combined with highly technical information. There are, however, useful chapters on corals, molluscs, fish and reef ecology. The book would be improved by the addition of maps and an index.

Sponges

185   **The burrowing sponges of Bermuda.**
       Klaus Rutzler.   Washington, DC: Smithsonian Institution Press, 1974.
       32p. map. bibliog. (Smithsonian Contributions to Zoology, no. 165).

Based on studies and fieldwork carried out between October 1969 and January 1973, Rutzler's work describes and illustrates the systematics and distribution of eight species of burrowing sponges. These sponges excavate limestone substrata to form burrows in which they live and participate in the processes of erosion and sedimentation. There are twenty-five black-and-white photographs and one table which gives the distribution of the sponge species at twenty-two collecting stations in Bermuda.

186   **An ecological discussion of the sponges of Bermuda.**
       M. W. de Laubenfels.   *Transactions of the Zoological Society of London*, vol. 27, part 1 (Oct. 1950), p. 155-201.

The author discusses the geology and climate of Bermuda and divides the island into six ecological subdivisions: the shallow, reef-studded region; the intertidal and coastal region; Harrington Sound; lakes; ponds; and enclosed bays and harbours. The study of thirty-three common Bermuda sponges is conducted in relation to these subdivisions and covers physical and chemical studies, sponge regeneration, sponge pigments, and the biological interrelationships which occur. A list of 233 West Indies sponges indicates which are found in the Dry Tortugas, in Bermuda, or elsewhere in the West Indies. Of the 233 listed, 65 are found in and around Bermuda.

187   **The porifera of the Bermuda archipelago.**
      M. W. de Laubenfels.   *Transactions of the Zoological Society of London*, vol. 27, part 1 (Oct. 1950), p. 1-154. bibliog.
The detailed descriptions of sixty-five species of Bermuda sponges in this article are of specimens collected by hand in shallow waters, just below low tide to a depth of five metres. The species discussed come from two classes: Demospongiae and Calcispongiae. There is an extensive bibliography.

188   **Bermudian species of Donatia (Tethya).**
      Blanche Benjamin Crozier.   *Annals and Magazine of Natural History*, 9th series, vol. 1, no. 1 (1918), p. 11-18.
Crozier gives detailed descriptions of three species of sponge: Donatia seychellensis, Donatia ingalli and Donatia lyncurium.

Hydroids

189   **Local distribution and biogeography of the hydroids (Cnidaria) of Bermuda.**
      Dale R. Calder.   *Caribbean Journal of Science*, vol. 29, no. 1/2 (June 1993), p. 61-74.
This study was carried out to investigate the local distribution, habitat species richness and biogeographical relationships of the hydroids of Bermuda and the nearby Challenger and Argus Banks, southwest of Bermuda. Calder found that species numbers are highest inshore in environments exposed to tidal currents and waves and offshore on deeper coastal substrates at depths between 25 and 100 metres. He also discovered that the diversity is lowest in sheltered bays and ponds; that Bermuda hydroids have a strong affinity with those of the Caribbean and the West Indies; and that endemism is low among Bermudian hydroids. An accompanying table (p. 66-68) lists hydroid species from Bermuda and their occurrence in a variety of marine ecological systems.

190   **Shallow-water hydroids of Bermuda: the Thecatae, exclusive of Plumularioidea.**
      Dale R. Calder.   Toronto: Royal Ontario Museum, 1990. 140p. bibliog. (Life Sciences Contributions, no. 154).
A systematic and nomenclature review of the thecate jellyfish of Bermuda collected at depths from the intertidal zone to 100 metres. Forty-six species from nine families, twenty-seven genera, are described and illustrated. Of the forty-six species discussed,

twenty-five are reported from Bermuda for the first time, thirty-seven are reported elsewhere in the western North Atlantic, and eighteen species are believed to be circumglobal in warm waters.

191 Shallow-water hydroids of Bermuda: the Athecatae.
Dale R. Calder. Toronto: Royal Ontario Museum, 1988. 107p.
2 maps. bibliog. (Life Sciences Contributions, no. 148).

A survey of twenty-six species in twenty-four genera of shallow-water jellyfish. Calder describes and illustrates each species in order to provide a taxonomic account of the athecate hydroids currently known from Bermuda to a depth of 100 metres. Of the twenty-six species discussed, twenty-three occur elsewhere in the western Atlantic, nine are circumglobal in warm waters, and eleven of the twenty-three previously known species are reported from Bermuda for the first time.

192 Additions to the hydroid fauna of the Bermudas.
Rudolf Bennitt. *Proceedings of the American Academy of Arts and Sciences*, vol. 57 (1922), p. 241-59.

Bennitt records and briefly describes thirty-seven hydroid species but offers no taxonomic discussions.

193 Notes on the hydroids and nudibranchs of Bermuda.
W. M. Smallwood. *Proceedings of the Zoological Society of London*, vol. 1910 (18 Jan. 1910), p. 137-45.

Describes three species in great detail: Chromodoris zebra Heilprin, Facelina agari and Polycerella zoobotryon. Smallwood's work is based on time spent in Bermuda in January 1909.

194 The hydroids of Bermuda.
Edgar Davidson Congdon. *Proceedings of the American Academy of Arts and Sciences*, vol. 42, no. 18 (Jan. 1907), p. 463-85.

Congdon describes hydroid species collected in the summer of 1903. Eleven previously recorded species are described generally while eight new species are illustrated and described in great detail.

195 On a few medusae from the Bermudas.
J. Walter Fewkes. *Bulletin of the Museum of Comparative Zoology at Harvard College*, vol. 11 (1883), p. 79-90.

Fewkes provides detailed descriptions of four Bermuda jellyfish: Agalma Okenii, Rhizophysa Eysenhardtii, Tamoya punctata and Oceaniopsis bermudensis. There is also a list of twenty-nine jellyfish species found in Castle Harbour, Bermuda in May and June 1882.

Seashells

196 **Caribbean seashells: a guide to the marine mollusks of Puerto Rico and other West Indian Islands, Bermuda and the lower Florida Keys.**
Germaine Le Clerc Warmke, R. Tucker Abbott.   Norberth,
Pennsylvania: Livingston, 1961. 348p. 21 maps. bibliog.

Warmke and Abbott provide information on periwinkles, conchs and other snails (Class Gastropoda); scallops, oysters and other clams (Class Pelecypoda); and squids, chitons and tusk shells (Classes Cephalopoda, Amphineura, and Scaphopoda). The text is accompanied by thirty-four black-and-white drawings as well as four colour and forty black-and-white plates. Each entry includes a description and distribution range as well as the scientific and common names.

197 **Bermuda shells.**
E. G. Vanatta.   *Proceedings of the Academy of Natural Sciences of Philadelphia*, vol. 62 (1910), p. 664-72.

Describes land shells collected in 1905, 1908 and 1909, and land and fresh water shells collected in 1910. Vanatta lists 187 shells found at 15 locations. Detailed descriptions accompany drawings for six new species: Physa caliban, Planorbis uliginosus, Planorbis imus, Ancylus (Ferrissia) bermudensis, Paludestrina bermudensis and Pisidium volutabundum.

Marine plants and algae

198 **Marine monocotyledonous plants of Bermuda.**
Albert J. Bernatowicz.   *Bulletin of Marine Science of the Gulf and Caribbean*, vol. 2, no. 1 (1952), p. 338-45.

Bernatowicz brings together and updates a number of scattered references to sea grasses and comments particularly on habitats and habits of growth. He confirms the existence of and supplements information about three species (Diplanthera wrightii, Cymodocea manatorum and Thalassia testudinum) and provides the first record for another, Halophilia baillonis. Bernatowicz is unable to confirm early records of the species Zostera marina. Finally, he describes the role of Thalassia colonies that promote sedimentation on the floors of bays by accumulating calcareous debris.

199 **The algae of Bermuda.**
Frank S. Collins, Alpheus B. Hervey.   *Proceedings of the American Academy of Arts and Sciences*, vol. 53, no. 1 (Aug. 1917), p. 1-195.

The authors first discuss previous collections of algae and provide information on the sites where the specimens they examined had been gathered. The bulk of the work is a description of 410 species: 342 marine species and 68 fresh water species. Of the total number, twenty-two species are new. A bibliography and thirty-nine black-and-white illustrations are included.

Birds

200 **A guide to the birds of Bermuda.**
Eric J. R. Amos. Warwick, Bermuda: Published by the Author, 1991.
206p. 4 maps. bibliog.

Amos has divided his work into two parts. Part one (p. 1-90) provides information on habitats, migration and locations of the birds in Bermuda. Part two (p. 91-199) contains descriptions of 344 species of bird found in Bermuda. For each species, Amos gives the English and scientific names; the months when the species is normally found in Bermuda; the number of years the species has been recorded in Bermuda; where the species is from and where it is on its way to; and the species habits and habitats. There are sixteen colour plates though not all species are illustrated.

201 **Ecological tinkering.**
Frank Graham. *Audubon*, vol. 86, no. 3 (May 1984), p. 38-41.

In the 1950s, David Wingate brought the cahow back from near extinction to thrive once again in Bermuda. This fascinating article describes his subsequent attempts to reintroduce the yellow-crowned night heron, a natural predator to the land crabs which were becoming a nuisance on Bermuda in the 1970s. The first chicks were from Tampa Bay, Florida in 1976 and by 1980 the first yellow-crowned night heron nests in modern times appeared on Bermuda.

202 **Bermuda petrel: the bird that would not die.**
Francine Jacobs. New York: Wm. Morrow, 1981. 38p.

Jacobs discusses the Bermuda petrel, also known as the cahow, which nests only in Bermuda. Although there were more than a million in Bermuda at the time of Columbus, the bird was thought to be extinct by 1620, until a sighting in 1901. This is the story of how the petrel was saved from extinction. It is written for young people and illustrated by Ted Lewis.

203 **Excluding competitors from Bermuda petrel nursing burrows.**
David B. Wingate. In: *Endangered birds: management techniques for preserving threatened species.* Edited by Stanley A. Temple.
Madison, Wisconsin: University of Wisconsin Press; London: Croom Helm, 1978, p. 93-102.

Wingate explains how he was able to protect the natural rock nesting sites of the cahow by designing a 'baffler' which allows the cahow to enter but which prevents larger birds (predators and competitors) from invading the bird's burrow. He also includes descriptions and illustrations for artificial cahow burrows.

204 **Bermuda's abundant, beleaguered birds.**
Kenneth L. Crowell, Marnie Reed Crowell. *Natural History*, vol. 85, no. 8 (Oct. 1976), p. 48-56.

Since 1945 there has been a decrease in native Bermudian songbirds and the native cedar had all but disappeared. Introduced species contributed to these types of reductions. This article describes the authors' studies of island birds since the late

1950s. The effects of development on birds and their habitats are examined. There is also a discussion of Bermudian flora and fauna prior to colonization and the types of species introduced over the years.

205 **Birds in Bermuda.**
Richard A. Slaughter. Hamilton, Bermuda: Bermuda Book Stores, 1975. 58p.

Slaughter's book is not a field guide to birds but rather an appeal, in words and photographs, for the preservation of the birds of Bermuda. Accompanying his text are forty-eight colour photographs and twenty-one black-and-white photographs. Slaughter provides information on migratory birds, the impact of humans on Bermuda and the conservation measures that have been taken. An appendix gives a brief summary of the nesting habits and survival states of twenty-two birds breeding in Bermuda.

206 **A checklist and guide to the birds of Bermuda.**
David B. Wingate. Hamilton, Bermuda: Island Press, 1973. 36p.

This work is divided into a short section of text and a much longer section consisting of a seasonal distribution and abundance chart. This chart lists 324 birds which can be found in Bermuda throughout the year. Wingate gives the frequency with which they occur and the abundance in which they may be found. The text contains information on resident and breeding birds, migrant birds, tips on finding birds in Bermuda, and descriptions of twenty of the more common birds found in Bermuda. This guide is indispensible for the serious birdwatcher who needs to know which birds are found in Bermuda and when is the best time to see them.

207 **First successful hand-rearing of an abandoned Bermuda petrel chick.**
David B. Wingate. *Ibis*, vol. 114, no. 1 (Jan. 1972), p. 97-101.

Wingate outlines the care and feeding regimen he undertook in 1971 to successfully wean an endangered cahow chick from its premature abandonment at eighty-four days old to its return to the wild one month later. He also provides detailed descriptions of the chick's growth and weight gain.

208 **Pleistocene birds in Bermuda.**
Alexander Wetmore. Washington, DC: Smithsonian Institution, 1960. 11p. (Smithsonian Miscellaneous Collection. Publication 4423).

Wetmore describes four species including, in detail, two new ones: Anas pachyscelus from the family of swans, geese and ducks, and Baeopteryx latipes from the family of cranes. Three black-and-white plates illustrate leg and wing bones.

209 **The breeding birds of Bermuda.**
W. R. P. Bourne. *Ibis*, vol. 99, no. 1 (1957), p. 94-105.

After providing a brief description of Bermuda, Bourne discusses the migrant and resident birds found on the island. There is also an investigation of the area's zoogeography, bird morphology and population, nest sites, breeding and reproduction, and the tameness of Bermuda's birds. The article concludes with an annotated list of the twenty resident species.

210   **New light on the cahow, Pterodroma cahow.**
       Robert Cushman Murphy, Louis S. Mowbray.   *Auk*, new series,
       vol. 68, no. 3 (July 1951), p. 266-80.

Outlines the early history of and early references to the cahow before commenting on
its present status. There are notes on the cahow's behaviour and its relations to other
birds and species. This article is based on observations of a small nesting population
discovered early in 1951. There are six black-and-white photographs.

211   **A list of birds recorded from the Bermudas.**
       Thomas S. Bradlee, Louis L. Mowbray, Warren F. Eaton.
       Proceedings of the Boston Society of Natural History, vol. 39, no. 8
       (Dec. 1931), p. 279-382.

The authors' introduction outlines early birding studies in Bermuda. The main list,
originally completed in April 1914, describes 232 specimens. The descriptions range
from one sentence to a complete page. A hypothetical list of fourteen specimens
which lack sufficient corroborative evidence to be included in the main list, is added.

212   **A comparative study of some subfossil remains of birds from
       Bermuda, including the 'cahow'.**
       R. W. Shufeldt.   *Annals of the Carnegie Museum*, vol. 13 (1919-22),
       p. 333-418.

Shufeldt's long report consists of correspondence on several collections of bones and
very detailed and lengthy descriptions of two new species (Puffinus mcgalli and
Puffinus parvus) and the cahow (Aestrelata vociferans), then believed to be extinct.
The article is accompanied by black-and-white plates (numbers 16-31).

213   **The bird-caves of the Bermudas and their former inhabitants.**
       R. W. Shufeldt.   *Ibis*, 10th series, vol. 4 (1916), p. 623-35.

Shufeldt describes the caves which he believes are no more than 500 years old, though
they may be even a century or less. The bones which were examined came from a
private collection and a collection housed at the American Museum of Natural
History. They are the bones of both shearwaters and petrels. Shufeldt describes three
new species, all believed to be extinct: Puffinus mcgalli, Puffinus parvus and
Aestrelata vociferans.

214   **The 'cahow' of the Bermudas, an extinct bird.**
       Addison Emery Verrill.   *Annals and Magazine of Natural History*,
       series 7, vol. 9, no. 49 (1902), p. 26-31.

The cahow, which the author believed to be extinct by 1625, was a web-footed sea-
bird unknown to ornithologists. It was nocturnal, could fly and run, and was tame and
unsuspicious of humans. The bird was the size of a pigeon, plover or partridge. It had
a strong, hooked bill and was russet brown in colour with a white belly. Much of
Verrill's article consists of extracts from *Historye of the Bermudaes* (see item no. 287)
written by Governor Nathaniel Butler about 1619, and unsourced material written by
William Strachey who had been shipwrecked on Bermuda in 1609. It transpired after
the publication of this article that the cahow was not extinct and there is now a nesting
population in Bermuda.

215 **The resident land birds of Bermuda.**
Outram Bangs, Thomas S. Bradlee. *Auk*, vol. 18 (July 1901),
p. 249-57.

The authors describe ten resident land birds. Seven of these species are indigenous (ground dove, Florida gallinule, crow, white-eyed vireo, bluebird, catbird and cardinal) and three (house sparrow, European goldfinch and bob-white) have been introduced to Bermuda by humans.

216 **The story of the cahow: the mysterious extinct bird of the Bermudas.**
Addison Emery Verrill. *Popular Science Monthly*, vol. 60
(Nov. 1901), p. 22-30.

Verrill uses quotations and excerpts from William Strachey (1609), Silvanus Jourdain (1610), Lewis Hughes (1614 and 1621) and Governor Nathaniel Butler (1619) to describe and speculate on the cahow which, at the time Verrill was writing, was thought to be extinct. Verrill concludes that the cahow was probably allied to the auks and was neither a shearwater nor any member of the petrel family. Later studies proved Verrill to be incorrect.

Insects

217 **An annotated checklist of the Coccoidea of Bermuda.**
C. J. Hodgson, Daniel J. Hilburn. *The Florida Entomologist*, vol. 74,
no. 1 (March 1991), p. 133-46.

The eighty-five recorded species of scale insects are listed alphabetically by family. For each species, the authors give the number of plant families and genera on which it has been observed; its current status in Bermuda; a brief history including attempts at biological control; and museums where specimens have been deposited. Of the species listed, two were responsible for killing up to ninety per cent of all the native cedars in Bermuda in the late 1940s and early 1950s.

218 **Annotated list of the Auchenorrhynchous Homoptera (Insecta) of Bermuda.**
Michael R. Wilson, Daniel J. Hilburn. *Annals of the Entomological Society of America*, vol. 84, no. 4 (July 1991), p. 412-19.

The authors list forty-three species of cicadas, spittlebugs, leafhoppers, treehoppers and planthoppers in eight families. The list includes twenty-six new records. Of these numbers, three species are considered endemic to Bermuda. Where known, the authors also note the insects' host plants.

219   The Lepidoptera of Bermuda: their food plants, biogeography,
       and means of dispersal.
       Douglas C. Ferguson, Daniel J. Hilburn, Barry Wright.   Ottawa:
       The Entomological Society of Canada, 1991. 105p. map. bibliog.
       (Memoirs of the Entomological Society of Canada, no. 158).

The 183 species recorded from Bermuda are discussed with respect to world
distribution, origin, long-range dispersal capability, host plants, nomenclature and the
circumstances of their occurrence in Bermuda. Of the species recorded, 59 are
reported for the first time, 125 are established residents, 50 resident species are
considered to be indigenous, and 11 species and 3 subspecies are endemic (one of
which is believed to be extinct). This item also contains information on the island's
natural history and physiography, together with an outline of the work of previous
researchers. An appendix (p. 67-77) by Ferguson is entitled 'An essay on the long-
range dispersal and biogeography of Lepidoptera, with special reference to the
Lepidoptera of Bermuda'.

220   **An annotated list of the true bugs (Heteroptera) of Bermuda.**
       Thomas J. Henry, Daniel J. Hilburn.   *Proceedings of the
       Entomological Society of Washington*, vol. 92, no. 4 (1990), p. 675-84.

The authors list forty-five species from fourteen families including nineteen new
island records. One indigenous species, Dagbertus bermudensis Carvalho and Fontes,
is described. All other species have been introduced from eastern North America and
the Caribbean. Available host plants and collection records for Bermuda, as well as
general distribution, are given for each species.

221   **The aphids and phylloxera of Bermuda (Homoptera: Aphididae
       and Phylloxeridae).**
       Manya B. Stoetzel, Daniel J. Hilburn.   *The Florida Entomologist*,
       vol. 73, no. 4 (Dec. 1990), p. 627-43.

The authors reported that there are forty-eight known aphid species and one
phylloxera species from Bermuda. This article consists of two lists. The first is an
alphabetical list of the aphids and phylloxeran with information on recent collections,
host range, world distribution and pest status. The second is a list of host plants of the
aphids and phylloxeran of Bermuda.

222   **The Coccinellidae (Coleoptera) of Bermuda.**
       Robert D. Gordon, Daniel J. Hilburn.   *Journal of the New York
       Entomological Society*, vol. 98, no. 3 (July 1990), p. 265-309.

Provides detailed descriptions and 120 illustrations of 14 beetle species including one
new species, Decadiomus hughesi. Discussions of distribution, host plants and
immature stages are included, along with keys for the identification of adults and
larvae.

223 **Hymenoptera of Bermuda.**
Daniel J. Hilburn, Paul M. Marsh, Michael E. Schauff. *The Florida Entomologist*, vol. 73, no. 1 (March 1990), p. 161-76.

The authors' survey of the bees, wasps and ants of Bermuda has resulted in a list of 199 known species representing 28 families. Twenty-five per cent of the species are either cosmopolitan or tropicopolitan, thirty-seven per cent are common to both Bermuda and eastern North America, and twenty-four per cent originate from the Caribbean region. Two species are known to be endemic and at least six remain undescribed. The listing gives minimal annotation or description.

224 **Annotated checklist of the Thysanoptera of Bermuda.**
Sueo Nakahara, Daniel J. Hilburn. *Journal of the New York Entomological Society*, vol. 97, no. 3 (July 1989), p. 251-60.

Thirty-eight species of thrips representing twenty-eight genera in three families are known to be from Bermuda. All except three species have been introduced from eastern North America and the Caribbean. Twenty species are reported for the first time for Bermuda. For each species the authors give collection data, a list of host plants and world distribution. There are also comments on the economic importance of several of the species.

225 **Annotated checklist of the whiteflies (Homoptera: Aleyrodidae) of Bermuda.**
Sueo Nakahara, Daniel J. Hilburn. *Journal of the New York Entomological Society*, vol. 97, no. 3 (July 1989), p. 261-64.

Ten species of whitefly representing seven genera are reported from Bermuda. Nine of the species have been introduced from the eastern United States and one species has been introduced from Great Britain. An eleventh species has not been found since the original collection was gathered and has apparently not been established in Bermuda. For each species the authors give collection data, a list of host plants and a general distribution. There are also comments on the economic importance of several of the species.

226 **Coleoptera of Bermuda.**
Daniel J. Hilburn, Robert D. Gordon. *The Florida Entomologist*, vol. 72, no. 4 (Dec. 1989), p. 673-92.

The authors' list of 228 species of beetle from 44 families includes 126 new Bermuda records. The list is arranged alphabetically by family, and then by genus and species within each family. They report that there are no known endemic species in Bermuda.

227 **Dragonflies of the Florida Peninsula, Bermuda, and the Bahamas.**
Sidney W. Dunkle. Gainesville, Florida: Scientific, 1989. 155p. 2 maps. bibliog.

A very good introduction outlines the anatomy and life history of the dragonfly, and provides information on photographing and collecting specimens. In the main body of the work, Dunkle examines ninety-four dragonfly species. Each entry includes a description and information on distribution, breeding habits, flight season, feeding, mating and egg laying. There are 127 excellent colour photographs and three checklists: for the Florida Peninsula, for Bermuda and for the Bahamas.

228 **Psocoptera (Insecta) from Bermuda.**
Edward L. Mockford. *Journal of Natural History*, vol. 23 (1989),
p. 1,177-93.

Seventeen species of Psocoptera, a type of winged insect commonly called psocids, are recorded from Bermuda. Four new species are described in detail: Echmepteryx atlantica, Caecilius bermudensis, Indiopsocus hilburni and Indiopsocus nebulosus.

229 **Spiders of Bermuda.**
Petra Sierwald. Wilmington, Delaware: Delaware Museum of
Natural History, 1988. 24p. bibliog. (Occasional Papers, no. 31).

Fifty-nine species from twenty-two spider families are known to occur in Bermuda. Sierwald has studied three separate collections as well as newly collected material gathered in July 1983 and May 1988. She gives a list of Bermudian spiders and provides a detailed description of a new species, Anyphaena bermudensis.

230 **The terrestrial arthropods of the Bermudas: an historical review of our knowledge.**
Douglas Keith McEwan Kevan. *Archives of Natural History*, vol. 10,
no. 1 (1981), p. 1-29.

Kevan reviews the recorded history of entomology in Bermuda from earliest times to the beginning of the 20th century. The first record of insects in Bermuda is found in a 1603 report by Captain Diego Ramirez. Kevan's section on the 16th and 17th centuries contains excerpts from a variety of sources. However, serious entomological interest began in the 1840s and 1850s and culminated in Angelo Heilprin's *The Bermuda Islands* (see item no. 121), the first published report of an expedition to study the area's natural history. An extensive reference list is included.

231 **The orthopteroid insects of the Bermudas.**
Douglas Keith McEwan Kevan. Ste. Anne de Bellevue, Quebec:
Lyman Entomological Museum and Research Laboratory, 1980.
182p. 11 maps. bibliog. (Memoir, no. 8) (Special Publication, no. 16).

Kevan's work is an 'annotated, systematic account . . . of the orthopteroid insect fauna of Bermuda Islands, including all the published references to each species that [he has] been able to see' (p. 6). This is a highly detailed historic look at the accounts of a variety of species including cockroaches, termites, katydids, crickets, grasshoppers and earwigs. An extensive bibliography (p. 139-55) and fifty-seven black-and-white drawings (p. 156-75) are included.

232 **Biological control of insect pests in Bermuda.**
Fred D. Bennett, I. W. Hughes. *Bulletin of Entomological Research*,
vol. 50 (1959), p. 423-36.

Prior to 1945, the small pest control projects in Bermuda were carried out by officers of the Department of Agriculture. They date back to 1875 when the Surinam toad was introduced to help reduce the number of insects, particularly cockroaches. This paper lists the natural predators which have been introduced into Bermuda and attempts to assess the fifteen species which have become established on the island.

233   **The folded-winged wasps of the Bermudas, with some preliminary remarks on insular wasp faunae.**
J. Bequaert.   *Annals of the Entomological Society of America*, vol. 22, no. 4 (Dec. 1929), p. 555-82.

Bequaert discusses both the ecological factors (climate and plant growth) and the geological factors affecting the distribution of wasps in Bermuda. There are also detailed descriptions of the three species of wasp present in Bermuda: Vespa arenaria, Polistes fuscatus and the new species, Odynerus (Stenodynerus) bermudensis.

234   **The Mediterranean fruit fly in Bermuda.**
E. A. Back.   Washington, DC: United States Department of Agriculture, 1914. 8p. (Bulletin of the US Department of Agriculture, no. 161).

Back's investigations of the fruit fly situation in Bermuda were made in December 1913. The fruit fly probably arrived from a ship in 1865 though it was not recorded in the literature until 1890. Back includes a brief life history of the fruit fly; a list of host fruits in Bermuda; a discussion of possible eradication; and a consideration of whether the Bermuda fruit fly is a source of danger to the United States. Back concludes that the fruit fly has spread over the entire Bermuda countryside, ruined the island's peach industry and discouraged other fruit growers. He also suggests that there is little danger to the United States, and that the fruit fly could be eradicated in three years.

235   **The diptera fauna of Bermuda.**
Charles W. Johnson.   *Annals of the Entomological Society of America*, vol. 6, no. 4 (Dec. 1913), p. 443-52.

Johnson lists ninety-five species of diptera (flies, gnats and midges), including eight new species. In this article, he has added considerably to the data that originally appeared in his 1904 article (see item no. 238).

236   **On the orthoptera of Bermuda.**
James A. G. Rehn.   *Proceedings of the Academy of Natural Sciences of Philadelphia*, vol. 62 (1910), p. 3-11.

The twenty-eight species of orthoptera (cockroaches, grasshoppers and crickets) recorded here were collected between December 1908 and April 1909. Only two of the species are peculiar to Bermuda; the others are also found in North America and the Caribbean.

237   **The ants of the Bermudas.**
William Morton Wheeler.   *Bulletin of the American Museum of Natural History*, vol. 22 (1906), p. 347-52.

The ant fauna of Bermuda is extremely meager. Wheeler lists eleven species with some comments for each. One new species, Prenolepis kincaidi, is described in great detail.

238   **A revised list of the diptera of Bermuda.**
      Charles W. Johnson.   *Psyche*, vol. 11 (Aug. 1904), p. 76-80.

The first recorded diptera species (flies, gnats and midges) from Bermuda appeared in 1859. Johnson's list comprises all previous records and provides brief descriptions of fifty species.

Mammals

239   **The taxonomy and status of bats in Bermuda.**
      Richard G. Van Gelder, David B. Wingate.   *American Museum Novitates*, no. 2029 (8 May 1961), p. 1-9.

Both the silver-haired bat and the hoary bat were first reported in Bermuda in 1884. Since then there have been reports of the red bat (1923) and the Seminole bat in the 1950s. The authors chronicle these reports and outline the status of bats in Bermuda. Only migratory and non-hibernating bats from eastern North America have been recorded in Bermuda. The seasonal distribution of bats in the islands follows the pattern of bird migration.

Invertebrates

240   **An evolutionary microcosm: Pleistocene and Recent history of the land snail *P. (Poecilozonites)* in Bermuda.**
      Stephen Jay Gould.   *Bulletin of the Museum of Comparative Zoology*, vol. 138, no. 7 (Dec. 1969), p. 406-531. bibliog.

An extremely detailed study of the subgenus P. (Poecilozonites) which is endemic to Bermuda. Gould's study considers all Pleistocene and Recent taxa of the subgenus and its evolutionary implications. There are five black-and-white plates and an extensive bibliography.

241   **Recent and fossil Bermudan snails of the genus Poecilozonites.**
      Henry A. Pilsbry.   *Proceedings of the Academy of Natural Sciences of Philadelphia*, vol. 76 (June 1924), p. 1-9.

Pilsbry describes ten species and subspecies of snail. Four of the species described are new (Poecilozonites acutissimus, Poecilozonites vanattai, Poecilozonites blandi and Poecilozonites gulicki) as is one of the subspecies (Poecilozonites blandi heilprini). He defines the snails as being isolated zoologically and deals chiefly with species found by Addison Gulick and E. G. Vanatta.

242   **The fossil land shells of Bermuda.**
Addison Gulick. *Proceedings of the Academy of Natural Sciences of Philadelphia*, vol. 56 (April 1904), p. 406-25. maps.

Gulick's descriptions of twenty-five species are based on shells collected in the summer of 1903. His descriptions include seven new species. The article contains three maps and thirteen illustrations (plate XXXVI, figures 1-13) follow the article.

Molluscs

243   **Vertical distribution of pelagic cephalopods.**
Clyde F. E. Roper, Richard E. Young.   Washington, DC: Smithsonian Institution Press, 1975. 51p. bibliog. (Smithsonian Contributions to Zoology, no. 209).

This survey is based on studies undertaken in the waters off California (1960-66), Bermuda (1967-71) and Hawaii (1969-70). The authors conclude that patterns of vertical distribution exist, based on and associated with maturity, diet and seasonal behaviour.

244   **The mollusca of Bermuda.**
A. J. Peile. *Proceedings of the Malacological Society of London*, vol. 17 (Dec. 1926), p. 71-98.

After providing a brief introduction to Bermuda and its land and marine molluscs, Peile lists 143 families of molluscs that are found on the islands. Only one species, Rissoina bermudensis, is described.

245   **On the Helicoid land molluscs of Bermuda.**
Henry A. Pilsbry. *Proceedings of the Academy of Natural Sciences of Philadelphia*, vol. 40 (1888), p. 285-91.

Pilsbry's study is based on shells collected by Angelo Heilprin in the summer of 1888. A general discussion of the Helicoid land molluscs is followed by detailed descriptions of four species: Poecilozonites bermudensis, Poecilozonites nelsoni, Poecilozonites reinianus and Poecilozonites circumfirmatus.

Crustaceans

246   **Ostracoda (Myodocopina, Cladocopina, Halocypridina) mainly from anchialine caves in Bermuda.**
Louis S. Kornicker, Thomas M. Iliffe.   Washington, DC: Smithsonian Institution Press, 1989. 88p. 7 maps. bibliog. (Smithsonian Contributions to Zoology, no. 475).

The authors provide detailed descriptions and illustrations of four species in four genera from suborder Myodocopina, four species in three genera from suborder Cladocopina, and one species in one genera from suborder Halocypridina.

247   **Benthic marine Cypridinoidea from Bermuda (Ostracoda).**
Louis S. Kornicker.   Washington, DC: Smithsonian Institution Press, 1981. 15p. bibliog. (Smithsonian Contributions to Zoology, no. 331).

Kornicker has reported on four species in four genera of benthic marine Cypridinoidea, including descriptions and illustrations of two new species: Sarsiella absens and Rutiderma sterreri. The two other species are Parasterope muelleri and Bruuniella species A which has not been formally named because only one juvenile specimen had been collected. Benthic marine Cypridinoidea had not previously been reported from Bermuda.

248   **Biological studies of the Bermuda Ocean Acre: planktonic Ostracoda.**
Louis S. Kornicker, Sheldon Wirsing, Maura McManus.   Washington, DC: Smithsonian Institution Press, 1976. 34p. bibliog. (Smithsonian Contributions to Zoology, no. 223).

Project 'Ocean Acre' is a group effort (the University of Rhode Island, the National Marine Fisheries Service, and the Smithsonian Institution) to make a comprehensive study of the biology and oceanography of the upper 1,000 metres of water within a one degree square southwest of Bermuda with its centre at 32 degrees North and 64 degrees West. Shrimp from this area were collected between 1967 and 1970. The authors have analysed migration patterns, habitats, distribution, stomach contents, and reproduction of two species, Macrocypridina castanea and Gigantocypris muelleri.

249   **Pelagic ostracods of the Sargasso Sea off Bermuda.**
Georgiana B. Deevey.   New Haven, Connecticut: Peabody Museum of Natural History, 1968. 125p. bibliog. (Peabody Museum of Natural History. Yale University. Bulletin 26).

Describes forty-three species of shrimp which occurred year-round, seasonally or only occasionally between 1958 and 1964, the period in which the studies were undertaken. The report also includes some quantitative data, especially on the vertical distribution of the commonest species. There are detailed descriptions along with sixty-two illustrations, three graphs and four tables.

250   **Harpacticoid Copepoda from Bermuda, part II.**
Arthur Willey.   *Annals and Magazine of Natural History*, series 10,
vol. 15, no. 85 (Jan. 1935), p. 50-100.

In this continuation of his 1930 article (see following entry), Willey describes thirty-four species including twelve new species in great detail. There are 188 drawings scattered throughout the text.

251   **Harpacticoid Copepoda from Bermuda, part I.**
Arthur Willey.   *Annals and Magazine of Natural History*, series 10,
vol. 6, no. 31 (July 1930), p. 81-114.

Willey carried out his fieldwork in the summer of 1928. Part I of his report describes in detail twenty-four species including six new species. There are seventy-eight drawings scattered throughout the text, and one black-and-white plate follows p. 114.

252   **Decapod Crustacea of Bermuda: I – Brachyura and Anomura.**
Their distribution, variations, and habits.
Addison Emery Verrill.   *Transactions of the Connecticut Academy of
Arts and Sciences*, vol. 13 (1908), p. 299-474. bibliog.

A discussion of the geographical distribution and origin of Bermudian decapod fauna precedes detailed descriptions for seventy-eight species, subspecies and varieties of crustaceans. Sixteen species had not been previously recorded from Bermuda, and nine species are described as being new. An extensive bibliography (p. 458-64) and twenty-eight black-and-white plates, which follow p. 474, are included.

Archaeology

253 **History and archaeology of HM Floating Dock, *Bermuda*.**
Richard A. Gould, Donna J. Souza. *International Journal of Nautical Archaeology*, vol. 25, no. 1 (Feb. 1996), p. 4-20.
HM Floating Dock, *Bermuda* was delivered from Great Britain in 1869 and eventually abandoned in 1908. Archaeological research began in 1986. Gould and Souza describe the initial research and the field trips undertaken in 1992 and 1993. They discuss the planning, construction and delivery of the floating dock; the history of its service; and its eventual disposal. The fact that parts of it still exist despite storm damage and dynamite blasts in the 1950s and 1960s is a testament to Victorian-era engineering and construction. Ten black-and-white plates, two tables of statistics and three sets of plans are included.

254 **History under siege: a review of marine archaeology in Bermuda.**
Jane Harris. *History News*, vol. 45, no. 4 (July/Aug. 1990), p. 15-16, 28-29.
The waters off Bermuda contain one of the Western Hemisphere's most valuable shipwreck graveyards available for the study of modern maritime history. Harris discusses the history of salvaging efforts, especially after the Second World War, the practice of modern marine archaeology which began in Bermuda in 1977 with the excavation of the *Sea Venture*, and the work of the Bermuda Maritime Museum. She also outlines the conflicts between the Museum, independent salvagers and treasure hunters.

255 **Excavations at Her Majesty's Dockyard, Bermuda.**
Jane Downing, Edward Harris. *Post-Medieval Archaeology*, vol. 16 (1982), p. 201-16.
Describes the 1981 excavations of the structural remains of two moats of the Bermuda Dockyard defences which date from the late 1820s. These excavations were part of a programme of work undertaken by the Bermuda Maritime Museum. The article contains three black-and-white photographs, four architectural plans, two cross-sections and five plans of seven mooring buoys which were found during the excavations.

256 **Seven nineteenth century buoys from H. M. Dockyard, Bermuda.**
Jane Downing, Edward Harris. *The Mariner's Mirror*, vol. 68, no. 4
(Nov. 1982), p. 411-20. map.

Seven buoys were found during archaeological excavations of the Bermuda Dockyard
in 1981. The authors describe three types of buoys in detail. One type is made entirely
of iron, the second of wood covered in zinc, and the third of wood covered in copper.
Eight black-and-white photographs, five drawings and a map are included.

History

General

257 **Shipwreck! history from the Bermuda reefs.**
Ivor Noel Hume.   Hamilton, Bermuda: Capstan Publications, 1995.
64p. 2 maps. bibliog.

Hume provides a very good introduction to the topic of shipwrecks and examines a variety of wrecks off Bermuda. He pays particular attention to the work involved in exploring them and recovering any treasure or artifacts which may be present. The book is well illustrated with colour plates.

258 **Bermuda recollections.**
Edited by Elizabeth J. Jones.   Hamilton, Bermuda: Ministry of Community, Culture and Information, 1993. 346p.

In 1988 Jones began conducting seminars at Bermuda College with seniors to discuss a variety of topics. Out of these seminars came many of the written memoirs in this work. The written memoirs have been supplemented with interviews conducted by Jones and the transcripts of some of the workshop discussions. There are sixteen interviews, forty-four written memoirs and nine workshop discussions. In the oral transcripts the grammatical errors have not been corrected, shifts in verb tenses have been retained, and the punctuation Jones has used reproduces the emphases, repetitions and pauses of the original speaker. This valuable historical and anecdotal record includes a number of black-and-white photographs.

259 **The story of Bermuda and her people.**
William Sears Zuill.   London: Macmillan, 1987. 2nd ed. 240p.
11 maps. bibliog.

This general outline of Bermuda's history from 1511 to the early 1980s attempts, as Zuill states in his introduction, to 'look at the Bermuda people as a whole, not as white Bermudians and black Bermudians' (p. viii). The book is divided into four major sections: 'Pre-settlement Bermuda', which covers the period up to 1610; 'The Archipelago', which deals with geography, flora and fauna, and climate; 'Story of the Bermuda People', which covers the period from the 1600s to the Second World War; and 'Modern Bermuda', which discusses the island's history from the Second World War to the early 1980s.

260 Heritage of Bermuda.
William Sears Zuill. *British Heritage*, vol. 5, no. 5 (1984), p. 10-19.

Zuill provides a readable but not overly detailed history of Bermuda from 1609 to the 1980s. This well-illustrated article is a good introduction to the topic.

261 A history of Bermuda.
William Sears Zuill. *The Magazine Antiques*, vol. 116, no. 2 (Aug. 1979), p. 320-27.

This concise history was written as an introduction to several other articles which make up an issue of *The Magazine Antiques* devoted entirely to Bermuda. The history is well illustrated with seven colour plates and twelve black-and-white photographs.

262 Bermuda's story.
Terry Tucker. Hamilton, Bermuda: Bermuda Book Stores, 1976. 211p. map.

This good, non-scholarly introduction to the history of Bermuda, first published in 1959, covers the time period from 1609 to 1975. Tucker, a prominent Bermuda historian, has also included a time chart from 1503 to 1975, placing Bermuda within a world context.

263 Bermuda today and yesterday 1503-1973.
Terry Tucker. London: Robert Hale; New York: St. Martin's Press; Hamilton, Bermuda: Baxter's, 1975. 208p. map. bibliog.

This general survey of the major events shaping Bermuda's history from 1503 to 1973 is an informative source of basic reference material and is an essential part of any Bermuda collection. There are seven useful appendices: 'Population Facts and Figures, 1609-1970'; 'Governors of Bermuda, 1612-1973'; 'Bishops, 1612-1969'; 'Principal Consular Officers of the United States in Bermuda, 1818-1972'; 'Sightseeing'; 'Forts and Batteries'; and 'Hotels and Guest Houses'.

264 Bermuda from sail to steam: the history of the island from 1784 to 1901.
Henry Campbell Wilkinson. London: Oxford University Press, 1973. 2 vols. map. bibliog.

Volume one covers the time period from 1784 to 1819 and highlights the building of the Naval Dockyard, the incorporation of St. George as a town, and the activities of the island's governors. Wilkinson discusses these activities in the context of the French Revolution, turmoil in the Caribbean and other world events. In volume two, which covers the period from 1819 to 1901, Wilkinson provides information on shipping, whaling, slavery, tourism and banking. Forty-seven black-and-white illustrations enhance the text.

265 **Notes on Bermuda military forces, 1687-1815.**
Rene Chartrand. *Military Collector and Historian*, vol. 22, no. 3 (1970), p. 73-79.

Chartrand discusses the succession of Great Britain's military forces in Bermuda from local militia to regular army and the Royal Marines. The first local militia was organized in 1687 by Governor Sir Robert Robinson. Chartrand outlines the importance of local militias, discusses the small garrisons of troops sent to Bermuda over the years, enumerates the provisions for the militia as outlined in various Militia Acts, and describes the uniforms of various militias and troops. There are also drawings of three uniforms: a private in the Garrison Battalion, 1783; a trooper in the Troop of the Horse, 1774; and a private in the Devonshire Parish Militia, 1812.

266 **Bermuda in the old empire: a history of the island from the dissolution of the Somers Island Company until the end of the American Revolutionary War, 1684-1784.**
Henry Campbell Wilkinson. London: Oxford University Press, 1950. 457p. map. bibliog.

This continuation of the author's *Adventurers of Bermuda* (see item no. 284) contains information on the first Royal Governor; pirates, privateers and smugglers; slavery, religion and schools; the town of St. George; and the American Revolution. This is an important and useful academic study of Bermudian history. There are nineteen black-and-white plates and appendices which list Government Councillors, Chief Justices, Attorneys General and Speakers of the Assembly.

267 **Bermuda (alias Somers Islands): historical sketch.**
J. Maxwell Greene. *Bulletin of the American Geographical Society*, vol. 33, no. 3 (1901), p. 220-42.

A good, early overview of Bermudian history from discovery in the early 1500s to the 1860s. Greene has included several excerpts from contemporary documents, and has based much of his article on Lefroy's *Memorials of the Bermudas* (see item no. 288). Greene also comments on topography, climate, architecture, industry and agriculture.

268 **An historical and descriptive account of British America.**
Hugh Murray. New York: Harper & Brothers, 1841. 2 vols.

The section on Bermuda appears in volume two, chapter six, p. 138-62. Murray outlines Bermudian history from the first discovery by Juan de Bermudez through the first settlement to the administrations of Richard Moore, Daniel Tucker and Nathaniel Butler. He also provides information on climate, agriculture, commerce and population.

17th century

269 **Survival strategies in early Bermuda and Barbados.**
Alison F. Games. *Revista/Review Interamericana*, vol. 22, no. 1/2
(Spring/Summer 1992), p. 55-71.
Games examines the success of immigrants to Bermuda and Barbados in the early
1600s based on the experiences of 983 immigrants to Barbados and 218 to Bermuda in
1635. She finds that although Bermuda offered a far superior lifestyle and greater
attractions, the immigrants to Barbados fared better in their new lives. In investigating
this apparent discrepancy, Games examines climate, government administration, the
type of immigrant each colony attracted and the average age of the immigrants.

270 **An introduction to the history of Bermuda.**
Wesley Frank Craven. [s.l.]: Bermuda Maritime Press, 1990. 2nd ed.
187p. 2 maps.
This early history of Bermuda from 1612 to 1624 examines Bermuda's role in the
New World, its form of government, plans for its settlement, the failure of those plans
and their subsequent revision. Particular attention has been paid to the Adventurers of
the Bermuda Company. This material was first published in the *William and Mary
Quarterly* (Series II, vol. 17, no. 2 [April 1937], p. 176-215; vol. 17, no. 3 [July 1937],
p. 317-62; vol. 17, no. 4 [October 1937], p. 437-65; and vol. 18, no. 1 [January 1938],
p. 13-63). The first edition, in book form, was published in 1938 by the author in a
limited edition at Williamsburg, Virginia.

271 **Colonising Bermuda – defending Virginia.**
C. Walton Brown. *History Today*, vol. 39 (Jan. 1989), p. 36-41.
Brown, a lecturer in politics and history at Bermuda College, presents arguments
which explain why colonizing Bermuda, in order to defend Virginia, made good
strategic sense. He also includes other examples of Bermuda's strategic importance in
the 19th and 20th centuries.

272 **The *Sea Venture*.**
M. L. R. Peterson. *The Mariner's Mirror*, vol. 74, no. 1 (Feb. 1988),
p. 37-48.
The *Sea Venture* was wrecked on Bermuda in 1609 and led to the island's settlement.
Peterson examines the history of another ship, the *Seaventure* or *Seaventer* which was
launched in July 1603. Although there is no proof that the ships are the same vessel,
the name is uncommon; three of the owners of the *Seaventure* (or *Seaventer*) were
members of the Virginia Company which sent the *Sea Venture* on its last voyage; and
there is no reference to the *Seaventure* (or *Seaventer*) being afloat after June 1609.

273 **European expectations of Acadia and the Bermudas.**
John G. Reid. *Histoire Sociale – Social History*, vol. 20, no. 40 (Nov.
1987), p. 319-35.
Covers the time period from 1604 to 1624 and examines the similarities and
dissimilarities between Bermuda and the Acadian region of eastern Canada. Reid

discusses the economic potential which English businessmen hoped to develop commercially in these two areas.

274 **Bermuda and Virginia in the seventeenth century: a comparative view.**
Virginia Bernhard. *Journal of Social History*, vol. 19, no. 1 (Fall 1985), p. 57-70.

Bernhard provides a comparative study of life in these two colonies with particular focus on social order and the leadership of the time. She suggests that: strong puritanical influences in Bermuda resulted in greater social discipline and the growth of stronger family ties than prevailed in Virginia; that greater religious strength was responsible for the significantly better treatment of slaves in Bermuda than in Virginia; and that a limited amount of space in Bermuda, along with the absence of any hinterland, compelled early settlers to evolve a sense of community which was not the case in Virginia.

275 **The Rich papers: letters from Bermuda 1615-1646: eyewitness accounts sent by the early colonists to Sir Nathaniel Rich.**
Edited by Vernon Arthur Ives. Toronto: University of Toronto Press, 1984. 413p. map. bibliog.

Sir Nathaniel Rich (c. 1585-1636) was one of the largest shareholders in the Bermuda Company. This collection of letters, which was published for the Bermuda National Trust, consists of ninety-seven well-annotated and footnoted documents sent by various early settlers to Sir Nathaniel. They provide an excellent insight into the lives and living conditions of the early colonists. There are several letters from Robert Rich (1586/87-1620), Sir Nathaniel's younger brother and one of the first settlers to arrive in Bermuda.

276 **Richard Moore, carpenter.**
Allen Mardis, Jr. *Virginia Magazine of History and Biography*, vol. 92, no. 4 (1984), p. 416-22.

Richard Moore, the first Governor of Bermuda, arrived from England in May 1612 and returned to England in the summer of 1615. Very little is known about Moore. Prior to his appointment he was a member of the Company of Carpenters Trade Guild and author of *The carpenter's rule*. Mardis uses 17th-century naval histories, shipwrights' company records, trade guild manuscripts and carpenters' company records in this interesting biographical sketch of Bermuda's little-known first Governor.

277 **Sir George Somers: a man and his times.**
David F. Raine. St. George, Bermuda: Pompano Publications, 1984. 189p. 3 maps.

The first complete biography of Sir George Somers (1554-1610), parliamentarian, navigator, merchant, adventurer and seaman. In 1606 Somers became one of the chief movers in the formation of the London or South Virginian Company for the colonization of Virginia. As admiral of the Jamestown, Virginia relief fleet of 1609, which was shipwrecked off the coast of Bermuda, Somers is the accredited founder of the island. This highly readable biography not only examines Somers' life but also the lives of those shipwrecked with him.

278 **The tempest.**
Avery Kolb. *American Heritage*, vol. 34, no. 3 (April/March 1983),
p. 26-35.

A vivid account of the final voyage of the *Sea Venture* which was shipwrecked off the coast of Bermuda in 1609 on its way to Virginia. Kolb relates the events which led up to the wreck and the subsequent period during which the survivors built vessels in which to continue their journey. He quotes from William Strachey's letter addressed to an 'Excellent Lady', probably the wife of a Virginia Company official. It is thought that the contents of this letter were adapted by Shakespeare for his play, *The Tempest*.

279 **Bermuda – unintended destination 1609-1610.**
Terry Tucker. Hamilton, Bermuda: Island Press, 1978. 92p. 4 maps.

Tucker's history of the unintentional founding of Bermuda contains contemporary accounts of the shipwreck of the *Sea Venture* in 1609 and the unplanned landing of Sir George Somers' relief fleet from England to Virginia. She has also included biographies of those people for whom Bermuda's parishes have been named and a brief Bermudian chronology from 1503 to 1612.

280 **Isles of devils: Bermuda under the Somers Island Company
1609-1685.**
Sister Jean de Chantal Kennedy. Hamilton, Bermuda: Baxter's;
London: Collins, 1971. 288p. 3 maps. bibliog.

This history covers both early Bermuda and the Somers Island Company, as it is difficult to discuss one without the other. This period in the island's history established the solid foundation for the country's future. Kennedy uses original letters, documents and archival materials as the basis of her research, and includes information on the legacies of the governors at the time, the influences of the rest of the world on Bermuda, religious persecution, the economy and the island's social conditions.

281 **A voyage to Virginia in 1609: two narratives, Strachey's 'True
reportory' and Jourdain's *Discovery of the Bermudas*.**
Edited by Louis Booker Wright. Charlottesville, Virginia: University
Press of Virginia, 1964. 116p.

William Strachey (1572-1621) and Silvester Jourdain (d. 1650) were both on the *Sea Venture* when it was wrecked off the coast of Bermuda in 1609. Strachey's account of the wreck (p. 1-101) takes the form of a long letter to an unidentified noble lady who, Wright surmises, was probably Lady Sarah Smith, wife of Sir Thomas Smith, treasurer of the Virginia Company. Jourdain's account (p. 103-16) was first published in 1610 in London by John Windet for the bookseller Roger Barnes. It was reproduced by Scholars' Facsimiles and Reprints (New York, 1940). Wright's work was published for The Association for the Preservation of Virginia Antiquities.

282 **The downfall of the Bermuda Company.**
Richard S. Dunn. *William and Mary Quarterly*, vol. 20, no. 4
(Oct. 1963), p. 487-512.

Dunn follows the personalities involved and the intrigue which surrounded the liquidation of the Bermuda Company by Charles II in 1684. He suggests that the downfall of the company demonstrates the Stuart aggression against corporate privilege and the British merchant class campaign to centralize Great Britain's empire.

283 **Bermuda's early days of adventure and colonization.**
Edith Stowe Godfrey Heyl. Hamilton, Bermuda: Department of
Education, 1959. 223p. 3 maps. bibliog.

Heyl's highly readable history was originally written to be used as a school text. It covers the time period 1511 to 1684, with an emphasis on the major events and personalities of the 17th century. She has included a time chart (1096-1687) and transcripts of some important correspondence. Despite its age, this history remains a useful source.

284 **The adventurers of Bermuda: a history of the island from its**
discovery until the dissolution of the Somers Island Company in
1684.
Henry Campbell Wilkinson. London: Oxford University Press, 1958.
2nd ed. 421p. bibliog.

This work, first published in 1933, traces the start of British colonization in the Americas and, in detail, chronicles the first fifty years of settlement in Bermuda. Wilkinson's study is well documented and includes a list of the Governors and Deputy Governors of the Somers Island Company (1616-84), a list of the Governors of Bermuda (1612-83) and a list of the island's Councillors (1612-84).

285 **The journal of Richard Norwood, surveyor of Bermuda.**
Richard Norwood. New York: Scholars' Facsimiles and Reprints,
1945. 163p. map. bibliog.

Richard Norwood (1590-1675) arrived in Bermuda in 1613, left in 1617, returned in late 1637 or early 1638, and remained there for the rest of his life. His journal, which he began in 1639, chronicles his life up to 1617 with some information beyond that date. This volume includes excellent introductions by Wesley Frank Craven: 'On Norwood's journal' (p. xi-xxxii) and Walter B. Hayward: 'Norwood and Bermuda' (p. xxxiii-lv). There is also a bibliography of Norwood's writings (p. lvii-lxiv) compiled by William A. Jackson, and Norwood's 'The description of the Sommer Ilands [sic], once called the Bermvdas [sic]' (p. lxv-xcii). The transcription of Norwood's journal (p. 1-111) is followed by a collection of Norwood's prayers (p. 113-30), an inventory of his estate (p. 131-43) and notes to the journal (p. 145-63).

286 **Lewis Hughes' 'Plaine and trve relation of the goodnes of God towards the Sommer Ilands'.**
Wesley Frank Craven. *William and Mary Quarterly*, 2nd series, vol. 17, no. 1 (Jan. 1937), p. 56-89.
First printed at London by Edward All-de in 1621, *A plaine and trve relation of the goodnes of God towards the Sommer Ilands* was written by Lewis Hughes (1572?-1655?), a Puritan minister in Bermuda, who arrived in the colony in 1614. Craven's introduction (p. 56-71) to Hughes' treatise provides a history of Bermuda's first decade and a detailed look at Hughes' life. Hughes' work (p. 72-89), heavily annotated by Craven, is an excellent history and description of the colony.

287 **The historye of the Bermudaes or Summer Islands.**
Edited by John Henry Lefroy. London: Hakluyt Society, 1882.
Reprinted, New York: Burt Franklin, 1964. 327p. map.
This manuscript is part of the Sloane MSS no. 750 held in the British Museum. Lefroy, a former Governor of Bermuda, assumes that the text was originally written by Captain John Smith of the Virginia colony. It describes Bermuda's early history from the wreck of the *Sea Venture* in 1609 up to 1620. The work records information on events and personalities and is an important addition to the Bermuda story.

288 **Memorials of the discovery and early settlement of the Bermudas or Somers Islands 1515-1685, compiled from Colonial Records and other original sources.**
John Henry Lefroy. London: Longmans, Green, 1877 (vol. 1); 1879 (vol. 2). Reprinted, Hamilton, Bermuda: Bermuda Government Library, 1932. Reprinted, Hamilton, Bermuda: Bermuda Historical Society, Bermuda National Trust, 1981. 2 vols.
This work, considered the definitive source for the history of Bermuda in the period covered, sorts, arranges and annotates scattered records of Bermuda. Volume one covers the period 1515-1652 while volume two covers the period 1650-85.

289 **Another account of the incidents, from which the title and a part of the story of Shakespeare's *Tempest*, were derived.**
George Chalmers. London: R. and A. Taylor, 1815. Reprinted, New York: AMS Press, 1975. 82p.
In discussing the sources for *The Tempest*, Chalmers outlines and chronicles the documents which tell of the discovery of Bermuda by the British in the early 1600s. This work contains excerpts from a variety of these sources.

290 **The history of the Bermudas or Summer-Islands.**
John Oldmixon. In: *The British empire in America*. London: J. Brotherton and J. Clarke, 1741. 2nd ed. Reprinted, New York: Augustus M. Kelley, 1969, p. 440-57. (Reprints of Economic Classics).
Oldmixon (1673-1742) gives an early account of the discovery, settlement and growth of Bermuda, with descriptions and comments on the climate, soils, agricultural production, and flora and fauna. This chapter also contains Edmund Waller's poem,

'The battle of the Summer-Islands', verses 'in praise of these islands' (p. 455). Oldmixon's work was first published in 1708.

291 The generall historie of Virginia, New-England, and the Summer Isles.
John Smith. London, 1624. Reprinted, Ann Arbor, Michigan: University Microfilms International, 1966. 248p. 3 maps. (March of America Facsimile Series, no. 18).

The first publication to claim specifically to be a history of English territory in the New World. Smith (1580-1631), head of the Virginia Colony in 1608, compiled an anthology of writings about Virginia, New England and Bermuda but, in keeping with the practice of the time, gave no credit to the original authors. At first thought to be a vanity piece, this work does, in fact, contain valuable information on early history. It is divided into six sections or books. The fifth book (p. 169-201) is entitled 'The generall historie of the Bermudas' and covers the time period 1593 to 1624.

18th century

292 Reverberations in Bermuda of the American Revolutionary War.
Terry Tucker. *Contemporary Review*, vol. 230, no. 1332 (1977), p. 32-42.

Tucker begins by setting the stage at the time: George James Bruere was governor and was having difficulties with his administration; food was scarce and had to be imported from the American colonies; and there was little agriculture being undertaken in Bermuda. Tucker discusses the Continental Congress' embargo, which put an end to trade with Bermuda, and an American theft of gunpowder from a magazine at Government House. She describes the influence of Loyalists on Bermuda and comments on a number of Bermudians who played a variety of roles at this time in the island's history.

293 Bermuda in 1776: Loyalist – or neutral?
Esmond Wright. *History Today*, vol. 26, no. 7 (1976), p. 437-43.

Wright discusses Bermuda's trade with the United States during the American Revolution, and the island's role as a refuge for Virginian families and British Loyalists.

294 The Andrew and the onions: the story of the Royal Navy in Bermuda 1795-1975.
Ian Stranack. Hamilton, Bermuda: Bermuda Press, 1975. 155p.

Stranack provides a very thorough history of the Royal Navy in Bermuda. He writes at great length about the planning, growth and eventual decline of the Dockyard established at Ireland Island. He describes the Dockyard in great detail and comments on the garrison's influence on island life. Appendices include pictorial descriptions of the naval property over the 180 years under consideration; a chronological synopsis of the history of the Royal Navy in Bermuda; and lists of officers at the station. The 'Andrew' of the title is a nickname for the Royal Navy and refers to St. Andrew, the protector of sailors. 'Onions' is a nickname for Bermudians and refers to the locally-grown Bermuda onion.

295 Bermuda's sailors of fortune.
Sister Jean de Chantal Kennedy.   Hamilton, Bermuda: Baxter's Book Shops, 1969. 155p. map. bibliog.

An in-depth study of Bermudian privateers who took advantage of the turmoil in the Caribbean as a result of the French Revolution and the uprising of slaves in Haiti. Much of the information in this book was originally published by the Bermuda Historical Society in four issues of the *Bermuda Historical Quarterly* (see item no. 528) (1959-60) under the title, 'Bermuda and the French Revolution'. The new material which was added for this book relates especially to the town of St. George.

296 The governor of Bermuda and the military garrison 1765 to 1768: a study of conflict.
Sydney W. Jackman.   *Journal of the Society for Army Historical Research*, vol. 46 (1968), p. 132-36.

Captain George James Bruere arrived in Bermuda to assume the post of governor in 1764. His term was marked by considerable conflict, particularly with his military commanders stationed in Bermuda. Jackman describes these conflicts in detail and examines conflicts within the executive branch of government.

297 Frith of Bermuda: gentleman privateer, a biography of Hezekiah Frith 1763-1848.
Sister Jean de Chantal Kennedy.   Hamilton, Bermuda: Bermuda Book Stores, 1964. 275p.

Kennedy examines the life of Frith, a prominent seaman and businessman who made and lost a fortune through his activities as a privateer. After the loss of his favourite ship in 1800, he settled in Bermuda where he became one of the island's leading legislators. In an appendix, Kennedy comments on the fortunes of the family following Frith's death. The endpapers carry a genealogical tree of the Frith family.

298 Bermuda and the American Revolution, 1760-1783.
Wilfred Brenton Kerr.   Princeton, New Jersey: Princeton University Press, 1936. Reprinted, Hamden, Connecticut: Archon Books, 1969. 142p. 2 maps.

This study of Bermuda's policies and role during the American Revolution is based almost entirely on manuscript sources. Kerr's aim is to 'investigate conditions in the non-revolutionary [British North America] colonies and suggest reasons for the attitude in each case toward the national movement in the thirteen [American colonies]' (Preface). As part of this study, he highlights prominent local personalities and examines their sympathies towards either Great Britain or the American colonies. Kerr also includes information concerning the activities of both the Bermudian privateers and the British Royal Navy.

299 **Relations between Bermuda and the American colonies during the Revolutionary War.**
Addison Emery Verrill. *Transactions of the Connecticut Academy of Arts and Sciences*, vol. 13 (June 1907), p. 47-64.
Verrill outlines the role of privateers commissioned to strike against the American colonies. He comments on American and French plans to capture Bermuda, and describes an important seizure of gunpowder from Bermuda and its subsequent importation to the colonies. There are also biographical sketches of Bermudian St. George Tucker (1752-1827) and Englishman George Ord (1741-1806), both of whom fought for the revolutionaries and played important parts in the relations discussed by Verrill.

19th century

300 **Rosabelle: life in Bermuda in the nineteenth century.**
Clara Frances Edith Hollis Hallett. Pembroke, Bermuda: Juniperhill Press, 1995. rev. ed. 124p.
Rosabelle Hollis (1850-1934) began her diary in April 1867 and continued it, with few gaps, until 1882. Hallett uses the diary as a basis for an entertaining and informative social history which provides interesting glimpses into the ordinary life, events and personalities of 19th-century Bermuda. Additional genealogical and historical information places the diary into its proper context. This work was first published privately in 1984 under the title, *Rosabelle, a diary of Bermuda in the last century*.

301 **Convict carvings: signs of sanity from Britain's infamous nineteenth-century floating prisons.**
C. G. Addams. *Sea Frontiers*, vol. 36, no. 6 (Dec. 1990), p. 40-45.
In 1828, 300 convicts arrived in Bermuda to construct a fortress on Ireland Island. Hundreds more eventually arrived and they were all housed in airless, floating prison hulks. Many convicts used the local limestone to carve chess pieces, crosses, talismans and pipes. The carvings, retrieved from the ocean floor off Ireland Island, are described and illustrated with colour photographs.

302 **Gibraltar of the west: Bermuda's Royal Naval Dockyard.**
Gail Huganir. *British Heritage*, vol. 11, no. 6 (Oct./Nov. 1990), p. 36-40, 74.
Traces the history of the Royal Naval Dockyard built in 1809 which, throughout the 19th century and into the early 20th century, was Britain's most important naval base in the Western Hemisphere. Huganir also describes restorations undertaken by the Bermuda Maritime Museum.

303 **Bulwark of empire: Bermuda's fortified naval base 1860-1920.**
Roger Willock. Somerset, Bermuda: Bermuda Maritime Museum
Press, 1988. 2nd ed. 159p.

Willock records the development in the 19th century of Britain's major naval base in
the west Atlantic and the fortifications which grew hand-in-hand with the new
dockyard. He describes the manner of the construction of the fortifications and the
tactics in their employment, and also evaluates the naval base's strategic significance
and its relationship to the development of Bermuda. Information is also included on
life in the garrison and the role of the Royal Engineers and the Royal Artillery in
building the fortifications which were to protect the dockyard from attack by the
United States. This well-documented treatise was first published by the author at
Princeton, New Jersey in 1962. This edition includes an index which the original
publication lacked.

304 **The Martello Tower at Ferry Point, St. George's Island, Bermuda.**
Edward C. Harris. *The Mariner's Mirror*, vol. 74, no. 2 (May 1988),
p. 131-39.

Martello towers were built as part of defence networks around the world from 1796 to
1873. The Ferry Point tower was built from local limestone in 1822. Harris discusses
the location, construction and defence role of the tower. One map, two black-and-
white photographs and five diagrams are included.

305 **The defences of the Bermuda dockyard.**
Edward C. Harris. *Post-Medieval Archaeology*, vol. 21 (1987),
p. 227-55. maps.

Although the Bermuda Dockyard was established in 1809, local defences were not
begun in earnest until 1820. Harris describes the evolution of these defences over the
ensuing century and gives some indication of the conservation and preservation
strategies for their future. The article contains three maps, ten architectural plans and
thirteen black-and-white photographs.

306 **American spies at Bermuda's forts, 1842-52.**
Edward C. Harris. *Post-Medieval Archaeology*, vol. 20 (1986),
p. 311-31.

Harris describes the visits of two American military officers, Captain Minor Knowlton
and Lieutenant Frederick Prime, to Bermuda for the purpose of spying on the island's
new fortifications. Both officers prepared reports on their findings. Harris expands on
the officers' observations by providing further information from a preliminary survey
of forts being undertaken under the auspices of the Bermuda Maritime Museum. The
article contains six black-and-white photographs and eight architectural plans.

307 **Sailing in Bermuda: sail racing in the nineteenth century.**
John Carstairs Arnell. Hamilton, Bermuda: Royal Hamilton Amateur
Dinghy Club, 1982. 255p.

Racing has always played an important role in the history of Bermuda. This book,
which marks the centennial of the Royal Hamilton Amateur Dinghy Club, chronicles
the events and proceedings of sail racing in the 19th century in great detail. Appendices

list major cup winners from 1861 to 1900, as well as every named Bermudian sloop and dinghy. Arnell includes size, owner, builder, race years and wins for each vessel.

308   **Old Bermuda: a collection of photographs of old Bermuda taken towards the end of the last century.**
       Bernard Wells.   Hamilton, Bermuda: Bernard & Caleb Wells, 1979. 52p.

This collection of forty-one photographs reproduced in sepia tones provides a good historic record of Bermuda from the late 1800s to the early 1900s. The captioned photographs include scenes from the Town of St. George's, the City of Hamilton, the Dockyard and rural Bermuda. There are also photographs of people.

309   **Governor Reid in post-emancipation Bermuda, 1839-46: an advocate of social and economic change.**
       Olwyn M. Blouet.   *Journal of Caribbean History*, vol. 9 (May 1977), p. 1-21.

Following the emancipation of slaves, Bermuda faced complex social and economic adjustments, and there were marked social and racial distinctions between ex-slaves and former masters. When Governor William Reid (1791-1858) arrived in 1839 there were few policies aimed at bolstering Bermuda's economy or aiding the transition from a slave society to a free society. Blouet outlines the situation in Bermuda prior to Reid's arrival and then examines Reid's energetic agricultural policy and his enlightened educational schemes. The article contains tables and graphs of figures for imports and exports, agricultural output, and the shipping industry for the mid-19th century.

310   **Horsewhips in high places: the turbulent decade, 1819-29.**
       William Edward Sears Zuill.   Hamilton, Bermuda: Hamilton Press, 1976. 128p.

This 'turbulent decade' was a particularly controversial time in Bermuda's history, a time of in-fighting and animosity between political dignitaries and church officials. In the early 1820s, the Governor, Sir William Lumley, and the Mayor of St. George's, John Till, were in constant disagreement. The involvement of John Lough, Rector of St. George's, exacerbated the situation which led to court cases in both Bermuda and England. By the end of the decade, Lumley had left Bermuda in disgrace and Till had committed suicide. This fascinating exploration of a small piece of Bermuda's history was originally published serially in the *Bermuda Historical Quarterly* (see item no. 528) in volume 14 (1957) and volume 15 (1958). The addition of a table of contents and, more importantly, an index would have been useful.

311   **Blockade runners of the Confederacy.**
       Hamilton Cochran.   Indianapolis, Indiana: Bobbs-Merrill, 1958.
       Reprinted, Westport, Connecticut: Greenwood Press, 1973. 350p.
       bibliog.

This very thorough description of the individual personalities and events around the blockade of the Confederate States during the American Civil War explores the important role Bermuda played as a commercial centre during this time. As the author points out, blockade running has frequently been cited as the source of wealth for many local families and, in fact, the port of St. George reached its peak of active commercial success at this time.

312 Confederate blockade running through Bermuda 1861-1865: letters and cargo manifests.
Edited by Frank E. Vandiver.   Austin, Texas: University of Texas Press, 1947. Reprinted, New York: Kraus Reprint Co., 1970. 155p.

Much of the material in this volume comes from the letter books of John Tory Bourne, a Bermudian merchant and Commercial Agent for the Confederate Government, stationed in St. George. Part one contains letters from four of Bourne's letter books (covering the period 12 August 1861 to 26 April 1865) and letters from a letter book kept by Major Smith Stansbury, Commander of the St. George's Confederate ordnance depot (covering the period 14 May 1863 to 2 November 1863). Part two provides a list of cargo manifests of blockade runners operating between Bermuda and the Confederate States from 22 April 1862 to 8 April 1865. An informative introduction establishes the context and provides historical information.

313 Bermuda and the blockade.
Charles Hallock.   *The Galaxy*, vol. 3 (15 April 1867), p. 890-99.

Provides a vivid description of the role Bermuda played in the blockade of the United States during the American Civil War. Writing soon after the events he describes, Hallock conveys the intensity and vibrancy of the times. The article subsequently appeared in the May 1892 issue of *The New England Magazine*.

314 Bermuda: a colony, a fortress, and a prison; or, eighteen months in the Somers' Islands.
Ferdinand Whittingham.   London: Longman, Brown, Green, Longmans & Roberts, 1857. 287p. map.

Whittingham (1814-78) arrived in Bermuda in 1855 and left the colony eighteen months later. In his account of the life of a British Army Officer on the island in the mid-19th century, he gives an informed view of the climate, health, history, education and religion, slavery, convicts and convict hulks, government and politics, social conditions and commerce. There are several appendices in which Whittingham provides statistics on import/export and trade (1838, 1844 and 1855) and annual rainfall (1852-56). There is also census information from the 1843 and 1851 censuses, and a discussion of yellow fever epidemics in Bermuda. The book, which according to the title page has been authored 'by a Field Officer', contains eight engravings.

20th century

315 Boer prisoners of war in Bermuda.

Colin H. Benbow. Hamilton, Bermuda: Bermuda Historical Society, 1994. 3rd ed. enl. and rev. 136p. 7 maps. bibliog.

Between June 1901 and January 1902, 4,619 Boer prisoners of war, ranging in age from eight to seventy-nine, were brought to Bermuda for incarceration and housed in six islands in Great Sound off Warwick Parish. Benbow provides descriptions of the camps, the treatment received by the prisoners, their daily routine and a variety of escape attempts. His information is based on archival documents, personal correspondence, reminiscences and interviews. There are extensive notes and forty black-and-white photographs in the text. Appendices include the personal reflections of one prisoner, August Carl Schulenburg (1879-1964); a description of the handling, censoring and distribution of the prisoners' mail; brief biographical sketches of twenty of the prisoners; and an additional forty-seven black-and-white photographs taken in the camps. The first edition was published in 1962 as Bermuda Historical Society Occasional Publications, no. 3, and the second edition was published in 1982 by Bermuda College.

316 Defence not defiance: a history of the Bermuda Volunteer Rifle Corps.

Jennifer M. Ingham. Hamilton, Bermuda: Published by the Author, 1992. 105p. bibliog.

The Bermuda Volunteer Rifle Corps (BVRC), for whites only, was established in 1892 and ceased to exist in 1946. Ingham's history of the corps is more personal than scholarly but still proves useful in recording Bermuda's past. Appendices include a list of officers, and BVRC members who served in the First and Second World Wars. The Bermuda Militia Artillery, which Ingham mentions in passing, was also established in 1892 and was for blacks only.

317 Canadian soldiers in Bermuda during World War One.

Jean-Pierre Gagnon. *Histoire Sociale – Social History*, vol. 23, no. 45 (May 1990), p. 9-36.

An account of the military and social lives of three Canadian infantry battalions (the Royal Canadian Regiment; the Canadian Expeditionary Force, 38th Battalion; and the 163rd [French Canadian] Battalion) which were stationed in Bermuda prior to being sent to Europe. The article emphasizes the social aspects of their garrison duty. Gagnon provides information on the selection of the battalions, their strength and composition, daily life in Bermuda and the way in which the soldiers were viewed by Bermudians.

318 Reminiscences of a Boer prisoner of war at Bermuda.

William Ayliff Cheere Emmett. *Africana Notes and News*, vol. 28, no. 1 (March 1988), p. 16-28.

Emmett (1859-1937) was taken prisoner in South Africa in 1901 and arrived in Bermuda after a month-long voyage. These notes are extracted from memoirs he wrote in 1935 at the insistence of his daughter-in-law. Emmett describes the voyage to

Bermuda and the return voyage in 1902, and paints a vivid picture of prison activities and prison food, the general treatment of prisoners and prison conditions during his incarceration.

319 **Defence outpost for North America.**
D. W. Buchanan. *Canadian Geographical Journal*, vol. 23, no. 3 (Sept. 1941), p. 106-15.

In 1940, certain areas of Bermuda were leased to the United States by Great Britain for ninety-nine years. Buchanan discusses the impact of this situation on Bermuda and particularly on St. David's Island which was most affected. The impact of the Second World War on the economy is also discussed. Eighteen black-and-white photographs accompany this article.

Local history

320 **The island that disappeared.**
Elizabeth Musson Kawaley. Sandys, Bermuda: Longbird Press, 1995. 128p. map.

This view of life in Bermuda in 1927 is based on the author's childhood memories of living on Long Bird Island. The island no longer exists as it became part of the main island of Bermuda when the airport was constructed in the early 1940s. The book is well illustrated with black-and-white photographs and is suitable for all ages.

321 **Lest we forget: they paved the way.**
Joy Cora Elizabeth Wilson-Tucker. Aurora, Colorado: The National Writers Press, 1990. 149p.

This volume introduces the people who have had the greatest influence on the small community of North Village. A local history with little reference to the history of Bermuda as a whole, it concentrates on individuals rather than events.

322 **Life on old St. David's, Bermuda.**
Ernest Albert McCallan. Hamilton, Bermuda: Bermuda Historical Society, 1986. 2nd ed. 258p. 2 maps. bibliog.

Although this is primarily the story of the author's boyhood, McCallan does offer a lively and anecdotal historical study of St. David's Island, the most easterly of the Bermuda group. McCallan comments on the people, food, craftsmen and tradesmen, homes and housewives, education and schools, churches, recreation and neighbouring islands. St. David's islanders are generally regarded as the direct descendants of Bermuda's earliest settlers. Intermarriage with visiting mariners and North American aboriginals has produced a separate and distinctive group of Bermudians whose general isolation from the rest of the country has produced a seafaring and agrarian sub-culture all its own. Although identified as the second edition, this is in fact a reprint of the original 1948 edition.

323   **The historic Towne of St. George Bermuda.**
      David F. Raine.   St. George, Bermuda: Pompano Publications, 1983.
      2nd ed. 55p. map.

St. George, Bermuda's first capital, was founded in 1612 and incorporated in 1797.
This is both a guidebook to and a concise history of the town. Raine has included
twenty-four black-and-white photographs and a list of mayors from 1797 to 1968. The
first edition was published in 1971.

324   **Biography of a colonial town: Hamilton, Bermuda 1790-1897.**
      Sister Jean de Chantal Kennedy.   Hamilton, Bermuda: Bermuda Book
      Stores, 1962. 400p. 2 maps.

This profile of the early growth and development of Bermuda's capital city helps to
illustrate the growth and development of the island in general. The information is
based on primary and archival material, and is an important source for understanding
the island's social and economic background. Appendices include lists of religious
ministers, Chief Justices, Attorneys General and Mayors; correspondence on the
Trinity Church fire; correspondence on the St. Edwards Church fire; and reports on the
negotiations for the lands comprising the city of Hamilton.

Genealogy

325 **Early Bermuda wills 1629-1835: summarized and indexed,
a genealogical reference book.**
Compiled by Clara Frances Edith Hollis Hallett.   Pembroke,
Bermuda: Juniperhill Press, 1993. 692p.

This alphabetical listing emphasizes the individuals named rather than the property
listed in the wills. Every name in every document is indexed, whether that name refers
to testators, family members, administrators, executors or witnesses. This invaluable
genealogical source takes its information from Books of Wills 1629-1835, Books of
Administrators 1782-1835, Volumes of Deeds 1677-1781, and Colonial Records
1616-1692.

326 **Early Bermuda records: a guide to the parish and clergy registers
with some assessment lists and petitions.**
Compiled by Archibald Cameron Hollis Hallett.   Pembroke,
Bermuda: Juniperhill Press, 1991. 443p.

Hallett compiled this valuable resource to aid in the location of genealogical
information in Bermuda. Each register book has been listed separately with an
annotation giving a biographical sketch of the writer, where appropriate, and a
bibliographical analysis of the book. Every baptism, marriage and burial record has
been listed alphabetically by surname with entries of the same surname listed
chronologically. Baptism records list the surname, the child's given name, the father's
given name, the mother's given name, the parish and the date of the baptism. Burial
records list the surname, given name and status (wife, widow, spinster, etc.) of the
deceased, the parish and the date of burial. There are two marriage lists: one
alphabetical list by the groom's surname and a second alphabetical list by the bride's
surname. Each marriage record includes the parish and the date of the marriage.

327 **The Jackson clan: the story of a Bermudian family.**
Vernon Jackson.   Hamilton, Bermuda: Published by the Author, 1991.
185p. 2 maps.
Jackson's family history begins with John Henry Jackson (1822-97) who established
the family in Bermuda. It spans eight generations, 185 years. Much of the work (p. 61-
184) details the life of the author who was born in 1907, but there is also useful
material about the earlier generations which provides some background information
about the social history of the island. The book includes a fold-out genealogical chart.

328 **Bermuda index 1784-1914: an index of births, marriages, deaths,**
   as recorded in Bermuda newspapers.
Compiled by Clara Frances Edith Hollis Hallett.   Pembroke,
Bermuda: Juniperhill Press, 1989. 2 vols.
An alphabetical listing of births, deaths and marriages as taken from microfilm files at
the Bermuda Library for the *Bermuda Gazette and Weekly Advertiser* (17 January
1784-31 December 1827) and the *Royal Gazette* (see item no. 522) (8 January 1828-31
December 1913). Where necessary, missing issues have been indicated. Volume 1
covers A to K; volume 2 covers L to Z.

329 **Bermuda settlers of the 17th century: genealogical notes from**
   Bermuda.
Julia E. Mercer.   Baltimore, Maryland: Genealogical Pub. Co., 1982.
276p.
Mercer gathers together abstracts of the earliest known records of Bermuda settlers,
much of it appearing to be from wills, and has listed the information alphabetically by
surname. This invaluable source was originally published serially in *Tyler's Quarterly
Historical and Genealogical Magazine* as 'Genealogical Notes from Bermuda' in
volumes 23-29, 1942-47.

330 **Notes on the Jones family of Bermuda.**
Lloyd Peniston Jones.   Paget, Bermuda: Published by the Author,
1947. 145p.
Jones began his work in 1925, intending to write a short history of the descendants of
Francis Jones, the founder of the family in Bermuda. His original work was based on
letters and papers inherited from his uncle and his father. The work grew to be a well-
documented genealogy, with references to and transcriptions of contemporary
government documents, from the first generation (Francis Jones, 1645-1709) to the
seventh generation (Edwin Jones, 1820-97). Jones also lists descendants up to the
eleventh generation. This work is both a historical and a genealogical resource.

Slavery

331 **Bids for freedom: slave resistance and rebellion plots in Bermuda, 1656-1761.**
Virginia Bernhard. *Slavery and Abolition*, vol. 17, no. 3 (Dec. 1996), p. 185-208.

Although Bermuda had the smallest slave population of any island colony, it did have its share of slave resistance. Six recorded uprisings and plots are all chronicled here in great detail. None of the Bermuda slave rebellions resulted in the deaths of any whites, although in the time period under discussion, nine slaves did die. Extensive notes accompany the article.

332 **Beyond the Chesapeake: the contrasting status of blacks in Bermuda, 1616-1663.**
Virginia Bernhard. *The Journal of Southern History*, vol. 54, no. 4 (Nov. 1988), p. 545-64.

Using original documents from the 17th century, Bernhard compares the treatment of blacks in Bermuda with those in the British colonies on the North American mainland. The discussion of such topics as family life, sexuality, trade and the possession of weapons demonstrates that Bermudian blacks experienced more tolerance when their daily life is compared to the harsher realities for Virginia slaves.

333 **The history of Mary Prince, a West Indian slave, related by herself.**
Mary Prince, edited by Moira Ferguson. London: Pandora Press, 1987. 124p. map.

Mary Prince, a slave in Bermuda, Turks Island, and Antigua, was born at Brackish Pond, Devonshire Parish in Bermuda around 1788. She was the first black British woman to escape from slavery and publish a record of her experiences. Ferguson's comprehensive introduction (p. 1-41) precedes Prince's text (p. 47-84), a supplement by the original editor, Thomas Pringle (p. 85-115), and four appendices (p. 116-24).

The history of Mary Prince was first published in London in 1831 by F. Westley and A. H. Davis.

334 Slavery in Bermuda.

James E. Smith. New York: Vantage Press, 1976. 314p. map. bibliog.

Smith's objectives are 'to trace the evolution of slavery in Bermuda and to examine its principle characteristics within the context of the colony's historical development' (p. 294). He also details slaves' legal rights and describes their social and work conditions. The work is divided into five time frames: up to 1685; 1685-1764; 1765-1800; 1800-20; and 1821-40.

335 Chained on the rock: slavery in Bermuda.

Cyril Outerbridge Packwood. Hamilton, Bermuda: Baxter's;
New York: Eliseo Torres, 1975. 226p. bibliog.

This thorough and descriptive account of slavery in Bermuda is supported by official statistics and contemporary documentation. Packwood investigates the living and working conditions of the slaves, the inequalities they endured and the legal rights they were given. He describes the conspiracies which were planned in order to escape bondage on the island.

Population

336 **Housing in Bermuda.**
Anthony Stukel. Hamilton, Bermuda: Bermuda Housing Corporation, 1994. 171p.

This first compilation of housing information from a variety of government departments is based on data from the 1991 census. The report has two main objectives: 'to present a systematic and exhaustive analysis of the housing situation at the time of the 1991 Census [and] ... to indicate the likely housing requirements during the current decade' (p. 2). The contents include data on and analysis of population, housing stock, housing issues and housing demand projection. Appendices include the 1991 census questionnaire, an outline of census concepts and definitions, and 114 tables of statistics.

337 **The 1991 census of population and housing.**
Bermuda. Census Office. Hamilton, Bermuda: The Office, 1993. 266p.

This document presents detailed findings from the 1991 census of population and housing. Specifically, it contains a report on the administration of the census; a discussion of concepts and definitions; sections highlighting significant findings related to the demographic characteristics of the population; labour force profiles; and major features of the households. There are two major sections of text and statistical tabulation. Section one (p. 2-83) combines text and seventy-seven tables covering such topics as population, fertility, health, birth, migration, education, the labour force, income, households and housing. Section two (p. 84-250) consists of seventy-two major tables taken directly from the 1991 census. Topics include age and sex, race and nativity, religion, education and training, economic activity and journey to work, the foreign-born population, marital status and fertility, households, housing and income. Appendices include the census questionnaire, the census organization chart, the census definition of Bermudian status, and previous population counts from 1911 to 1980.

338 **Report of the population census 1980.**
Bermuda. Census Office. Hamilton, Bermuda: The Office, 1980.
543p.

Provides statistics from the census held on 12 May 1980. The first three chapters outline the administration of the census, the concepts and definitions used, and the census questionnaire. Chapter four, also issued as a separate volume, presents a summary of the findings, and chapter five (p. 81-520) contains the tabular findings. There are sixty-eight tables of statistics covering population, economic activity, nativity, internal migration, education and training, race and religion, marital status and fertility, and households and rent.

339 **Report of the population census 1970.**
Bermuda. Census Office. Hamilton, Bermuda: The Office, 1973.
265p.

Provides statistics for population, households and families, age, race and religion, marital status, migration, education and training, fertility, economic activity and housing. Chapters one to three outline the administration of the census, describe the concepts and definitions used, and describe the tables of statistics. Chapter four gives a summary of the findings while the bulk of the work (p. 49-232) contains the sixty-eight detailed statistical tables.

340 **Population dynamics of Bermuda: a decade of change.**
Dorothy K. Newman. Hamilton, Bermuda: Ministry of Finance,
1972. 180p. bibliog.

Newman provides a summary analysis of the 1970 census of Bermuda (see item no. 339) and a preliminary review intended to assist with government planning and policy determinations. She also examines population changes from 1960 to 1970 in twenty-four pages of text and fifty-nine tables of statistics.

341 **Census of Bermuda 23rd October, 1960.**
Bermuda. Census Office. Hamilton, Bermuda: The Office, 1961.
136p.

Fifty-six tables, with minimal text, list statistics on population and housing.

Folklore

342 Bermuda's favourite haunts.
John Cox, Mac Musson, Joan Skinner.   Flatts, Bermuda: Ghost
Writers, 1991 (vol. 1); 1996 (vol. 2).
Most of the tales of Bermudian ghosts, superstitions, myths and fallacies in these two
volumes centre around a particular house or building. There are forty tales in volume
one and another thirty-four in volume two, which is subtitled 'picking up the threads'.
All of the stories are based on either eye-witness accounts or traditional folklore.

**343 Bermuda and the supernatural: superstitions and beliefs from
17th-20th centuries.**
Terry Tucker.   Hamilton, Bermuda: Island Press, 1968. 176p.
Tucker's work contains stories and information on apparitions, astrology, buried
treasure, haunted houses, herbal remedies and love potions. She also examines twenty-
two witchcraft trials, including six convictions and one reprieve.

344 Bermuda folklore.
Elsie Worthington Clews Parsons.   *Journal of American Folk-Lore*,
vol. 38, no. 148 (April-June 1925), p. 239-66.
Parsons' collection of folklore includes six tales, four proverbs, seven rhymes and 162
riddles plus variants on those riddles. There is also information on miscellaneous
practices and beliefs including the traditions of flying kites on Good Friday and
serving cassava pie at Christmas.

Religion

345 Chronicle of a colonial church: 1612-1826, Bermuda.
Archibald Cameron Hollis Hallett. Pembroke, Bermuda: Juniperhill
Press, 1993. 420p. 2 maps.

This thorough history of religion and the churches in Bermuda is also a general social
history and a history of education (1612-1840). Hallett provides detailed information
for all parishes and churches based on primary government and parish sources, the
majority of which are housed in the Bermuda Archives. Appendices list clergy
assignments from 1612 to 1840, provide information on civil and parish government
from 1612 to 1830, and outline the services and ministrations provided by the church
in Bermuda.

346 On this rock: a photographic essay on the churches of Bermuda.
Thornton M. Henry. Oakville, Ontario, Canada: Carter & Carter,
1993. 143p. map.

Bermuda has more churches per square mile than any other country. Henry's 187
excellent colour photographs highlight 83 churches. The commentary provides
historical details about the individual churches and the denominations they represent.

347 From rocks and ice to leafy isles: Bermuda's links with the
Dioceses of Nova Scotia and Newfoundland.
Robert Hamilton Hubbard. *Journal of the Canadian Church
Historical Society*, vol. 29, no. 1 (April 1987), p. 3-11.

Focuses on the 19th and early 20th century links between the Church of England's
dioceses and Bermuda. Hubbard describes the work of John Inglis, Bishop of Nova
Scotia and its Dependencies (1825-39), Aubrey Spencer, Bishop of Newfoundland
with Bermuda (1839-43) and Edward Feild, Bishop of Newfoundland with Bermuda
(1844-76). Hubbard also includes information about Llewellyn Jones, Bishop of
Newfoundland with Bermuda (1878-1917) and Arthur Heber Browne who became the
first Bishop of Bermuda in 1925.

348 **The Roman Catholic Archdiocese of Halifax and the Colony of Bermuda, 1832-1953.**
Robert Nicholas Berard. *Collections of the Royal Nova Scotia Historical Society*, vol. 42 (1986), p. 121-38.

The first priests who were sent to Bermuda from Halifax during the 1830s and 1840s left soon after their arrival. It was not until the late 1840s that Roman Catholic priests tended to stay (and were allowed to stay) longer than six months. Berard discusses the church's trials and tribulations during the 19th and early 20th century, church politics in the 1930s, and church expansion in the 1940s. He also examines the themes that pervade the Church's history to 1953: the difficulties in administering the church from Halifax; the church's economic struggles; the shortage of priests; communication challenges; and cultural differences.

349 **Bermuda: our warmest presbytery.**
Mike Milne. *The United Church Observer*, new series, vol. 48, no. 11 (May 1985), p. 14-17.

When Milne wrote this article, there were 40 denominations and 100 churches in Bermuda. The eight Methodist congregations upon which he focuses were members of the Bermuda Synod, part of the Maritime Conference in the United Church of Canada (UCC). Although there was a strong Bermudian lay leadership, the clergy were all non-Bermudian. Milne comments on social conditions, and the lay leadership's alienation and isolation from the UCC.

350 **Maritime Methodists and black Bermudians, 1851-1870.**
Graeme S. Mount. *Nova Scotia Historical Review*, vol. 4, no. 2 (1984), p. 39-50.

After 1800, many black Bermudians joined the Methodist Church. However, the clergy, who had strong ties to Nova Scotia and New Brunswick, had difficulty overcoming their prejudices concerning blacks. Mount shows how the clergy's acceptance of the Bermudian status quo and its practice of racial segregation prompted the movement of many blacks into the British Methodist Episcopal Church after 1870.

351 **The missing Mr. Read: the story of Bermuda Adventists.**
Nellie Eileen Musson. Toronto: University of Toronto Press, 1984. 215p.

Francis Read, about whom little is known, introduced the Seventh Day Adventist movement into Bermuda. Musson provides an introduction to the movement and outlines its growth on the island from 1869. She also provides a great deal of information about individuals prominent in the church.

352 **Presbyterians in Bermuda.**
Warwick, Bermuda: Kirk Session of Christ Church, 1984. 185p.

This collection of articles, all previously published elsewhere, focuses on the impact of the congregation of Christ Church on the entire community. The articles are 'Presbyterianism in Bermuda: early religious history' by Peter J. C. Smith; 'The early Bermuda church' by William Robson Notman; 'Reminiscences of an old Bermuda church' by Joseph H. S. Frith; 'A short sketch of Christ Church' by E. A. McCallan;

'A guide to Christ Church history' by Esther K. Law; and 'Christ Church, Warwick, 1960-1984' by Archibald Notman Smith. The book is well illustrated with black-and-white photographs.

353   **Bishop John Inglis and his attitude towards race in Bermuda in the era of emancipation.**
Graeme S. Mount, Joan E. Mount.   *Journal of the Canadian Church Historical Society*, vol. 25, no. 1 (April 1983), p. 25-32.

John Inglis was Bishop of Nova Scotia from 1825 to 1839, during which time Bermuda came under his charge. The authors examine Inglis' liberal attitudes towards race and his policies to promote education for blacks and to encourage their membership in the church. Even prior to emancipation, Inglis insisted that slave and master attend church together, a policy which resulted in a remarkable degree of integration in the years which followed the abolition of slavery in Bermuda.

354   **Friends in Bermuda in the seventeenth century.**
A. Day Bradley.   *Journal of the Friends' Historical Society*, vol. 54, no. 1 (1976), p. 3-11.

Quakerism reached Bermuda in February 1660 with the arrival of Richard Pinder and George Rose but there is little indication that it survived into the 18th century. Since the movement was never strong in Bermuda, records are hard to come by; however, Bradley has managed to collect information from a number of scattered sources in order to comment on the discrimination against Quakers in Bermuda during these early years.

355   **The narrative of a mission to Nova Scotia, New Brunswick, and the Somers Islands.**
Joshua Marsden.   New York: Johnson Reprint, 1966. 289p.

Marsden was a Methodist missionary to Nova Scotia and New Brunswick (1800-08) and Bermuda (1808-14). His account of the missions to and his own work in Bermuda appears in chapters nine to eleven (p. 114-70). Chapter nine contains background information about Bermuda and an account of the missionary, John Stephenson, who was sent to Bermuda in 1799. Chapter eleven concludes with Marsden's poem, 'A descriptive epistle from Bermuda' (p. 163-70). Appendices provide information on Methodist missions from 1770 to 1815.

356   **The church in Bermuda: a brief sketch.**
John Stow.   Toronto: The Canadian Church Historical Society, 1957. 16p. (Occasional Publication, no. 1).

This history of the Church of England in Bermuda covers the period from the first services which were conducted for the survivors of the *Sea Venture* in 1609 up to the 1950s. Despite his emphasis on the Church of England, Stow also discusses other denominations. The text contains numerous excerpts from a variety of contemporary documents and sermons. At the time of writing, Stow was Rector of St. George's Parish and Archdeacon of Bermuda.

357 **Bermuda's priests: the history of the establishment and growth of the Catholic Church in Bermuda.**
John M. McCarthy. Quebec City: P. Larose, 1954. 151p. map.

This detailed history of the Catholic Church in Bermuda covers the period from the arrival of the first Catholic resident in 1656 up to the 1950s. The work, begun in 1944 at the request of the Archbishop of Halifax, first appeared as a series of articles in the *Church Bulletin*. It comprises a general history of the Catholic Church in Bermuda but also includes histories of individual churches on the island. An appendix lists bishops and archbishops (1817-1952) and priests stationed in Bermuda (1832-1953).

358 **Methodism in Bermuda.**
D. W. Johnson. In: *History of Methodism in Eastern British America*. Sackville, New Brunswick, Canada: Tribune Printing Co., 1926?, p. 348-63.

Johnson relates the history of Methodism in Bermuda beginning with the arrival of the first missionary in 1799. The first Methodist church was built in 1810. This detailed history includes names, dates, and accomplishments, and concludes with a list of pastors from 1855 to 1925.

359 **The early Bermuda church.**
William Robson Notman. *The Presbyterian and Reformed Review*, vol. 7 (Oct. 1896), p. 630-47.

This history of the Presbyterian Church in Bermuda is written in 'an attempt to claim justice for the Presbyterian Church in Bermuda . . . [and to highlight its part] in the early religious history of the colony' (p. 630). Notman also hopes to correct Lefroy's study of religion in *The historye* [sic] *of the Bermudaes* [sic] *or Summer* [sic] *Islands* (see item no. 287). In particular, Notman refutes Lefroy's claims that the Church of England was established in Bermuda from the founding of the colony in 1612; that the first ministers were from the Church of England; and that Presbyterianism was not established in Bermuda prior to 1652.

360 **History of the Methodist Church within the territories embraced in the late conference of eastern British America, including Nova Scotia, New Brunswick, Prince Edward Island and Bermuda.**
Thomas Watson Smith. Halifax, Nova Scotia, Canada: Methodist Book Room, 1877 (vol. 1), 1890 (vol. 2).

In volume one, two chapters outline the history of the Methodist Church in Bermuda: 'Methodism in Bermuda, from the arrival of John Stephenson in 1799, to his departure in 1802' (p. 439-64); and 'Methodism in Bermuda, from the departure of John Stephenson in 1802, to the summer of 1813' (p. 465-91). There are also two pertinent chapters in volume two: 'Methodism in Bermuda, from 1813 to the centenary celebration in 1839' (p. 133-62); and 'Methodism in Bermuda, from the centenary celebration of 1839 to formation of Eastern British American conference in 1855' (p. 374-84).

Social Conditions

361 **Bermuda's stride toward the twenty-first century.**
Dorothy K. Newman.   Hamilton, Bermuda: Statistical Department,
Ministry of Finance, 1994. 102p. bibliog.
Newman's socio-economic study examines population distribution and mobility, work, Bermudianization and aspects of the standard of living in Bermuda. She hopes that it will contribute to the government's policy planning. Sixty tables of statistics are included.

362 **Gladys Morrell and the women's suffrage movement in Bermuda.**
Colin H. Benbow.   Warwick, Bermuda: The Writers' Machine, 1994.
82p.
This combined biography of Gladys De Courcy Morrell (1888-1969) and history of the development of the Bermuda Woman's Suffrage Society evaluates and reviews the events and personalities involved in achieving the vote for women in Bermuda in 1943. Appendices include eighteen biographical sketches of some of the personalities involved; the 1923 Constitution of the Bermuda Woman's Suffrage Society; a list of female 'firsts' in politics from 1945 to 1993; and a list of women who have sat in the Legislature of Bermuda.

363 **Paradise found, – almost!: a collection of writings (in chronological order).**
Vernon Jackson.   Hamilton, Bermuda: Globe Press, 1994. 234p.
Contains Jackson's letters to the editor, recollections and poems written between 1931 and 1994. Many of the pieces originally appeared in *The Royal Gazette* (see item no. 522) and *The Mid-Ocean News* (see item no. 521). Topics include history, politics, people, the police service, entertainment, education, crime, health and social concerns.

364 **Saturday's children: from London workhouse to Bermuda indenture 1850: a journey from darkness into light.**
Jocelyn Motyer Raymond.   Pembroke, Bermuda: Arrowroot Press, 1994. 172p. bibliog.

Raymond chronicles the lives of children who volunteered to be taken from a St. Pancras parish workhouse in London in 1849 and 1850 and sent to live and work in Bermuda. This description of the successful venture was thoroughly researched: the text includes numerous quotations from the children's letters as well as material from contemporary archival documents. Appendices list the dates when the children were sent and on what ship, their ages at the time of emigration, and the name of the individual in Bermuda to whom they were sent.

365 **Transitions: voices of Bermudian women.**
Edited by Dale Butler.   Warwick, Bermuda: The Writers' Machine, 1994. 91p.

A collection of timely and thoughtful essays by eleven women, spanning the spectrum of age, race and social class. They include health professionals, businesswomen, politicians, writers, a teacher and a lawyer. Their essays all deal with pressing social concerns relevant to Bermuda.

366 **Social integration and caregiving among seniors in Bermuda.**
Neena L. Chappell, Victor W. Marshall.   *Ageing and Society*, vol. 12 (1992), p. 499-514.

The authors examine the social interaction among Bermudian seniors; the relationship of various interaction variables with the seniors' psychological and emotional well-being; and the caregiving the seniors receive. Chappell and Marshall reach several conclusions: that Bermudian seniors have strong social ties; that perceived health is related to life satisfaction; that functional disability is related to self-esteem; that informal assistance is strong; and that the geographical isolation and small size of the island is related to a strong social network.

367 **Commentary: some '*Sun*' essays.**
Colin H. Benbow.   Hamilton, Bermuda: Island Press, 1991. 88p.

A collection of 66 essays from the more than 150 written by the author for the *Bermuda Sun* (see item no. 520) between 1988 and 1991. Some of the topics are international in their subject matter: the downfall of Communism; the re-unification of Germany; AIDS; and the Gulf War. However, many of the essays tackle specifically Bermudian topics such as educational reform, overcrowding on the island, drugs, elections, the economic recession, tourism and unemployment.

368 **The other side (looking behind the shield).**
Larry Burchall.   Detroit, Michigan: Harlo Press, 1991. 119p. bibliog.

This irreverent, tongue-in-cheek volume, harsh but honest, discusses social conditions in Bermuda. Burchall examines social customs, government, tourism, racism, expatriates, crime and punishment, morality, the economy, and male and female relationships.

369 **The socioeconomics of a female majority in eighteenth-century Bermuda.**
Elaine Forman Crane. *Signs: Journal of Women in Culture and Society*, vol. 15, no. 2 (Winter 1990), p. 231-58.

Basing much of her work on research conducted using land and inheritance records for 1622-1779, Crane demonstrates that a shortage of males in Bermuda during that period presented white women with certain distinct advantages. Demographic information reveals that white Bermudian females owned more property than their mainland counterparts, and that they inherited more land than the white males. With property and a highly visible degree of influence in the world of commerce, these women enjoyed a far greater economic independence than female colonists elsewhere.

370 **Caregivers in day-care centers: does training matter?**
Jeffrey Arnett. *Journal of Applied Developmental Psychology*, vol. 10, no. 4 (Oct.-Dec. 1989), p. 541-52.

Arnett studies fifty-nine caregivers in twenty-two day-care centres in Bermuda to determine how training is related to both caregivers' childrearing attitudes and their behaviour towards the children in their care. He concludes that caregivers with training are less authoritarian in their childrearing attitudes and enjoy more positive interaction with the children in their care.

371 **Far from home: an experimental evaluation of the Mother-Child Home Program in Bermuda.**
Sandra Scarr, Kathleen McCartney. *Child Development*, vol. 59, no. 3 (June 1988), p. 531-43.

The Mother-Child Home Program, developed in the United States, employs home visitors who demonstrate for mothers the many ways to interact more positively with their young children and to provide more educational experiences for them. This article evaluates the programme in Bermuda with a broad range of measures on cognitive, social and emotional development. The authors report that children in the Bermuda programme scored above US norms on cognitive tests and were functioning well in the pre-school period.

372 **Second class citizens, first class men.**
Eva Naomi Hodgson. Hamilton, Bermuda: The Writers' Machine, 1988. 2nd ed. 273p.

This useful and oft-cited work outlines the social history of Bermuda from 1953 to 1963, a time when desegregation took place, labour unions were formed, black political parties were formed, and the franchise was extended to all Bermudians over the age of twenty-one. The first edition was sponsored by the Amalgamated Bermuda Union of Teachers in 1967. In this second edition, Hodgson updates the fight for equality for the black population to the 1980s.

373 **Child-care quality and children's social development.**
Deborah Phillips, Kathleen McCartney, Sandra Scarr. *Developmental Psychology*, vol. 23, no. 4 (1987), p. 537-43.

Examines the influence of child-care environments on children's social development. The authors conclude that overall quality, caregiver-child verbal interactions, and director experience are each highly predictive of the children's social development. Child-care experience shows few significant effects. Bermuda was chosen for this study because approximately eighty-five per cent of Bermudian children spend the majority of their day in some form of substitute care by the time they are two years old, and because Bermuda child-care programmes are remarkably stable and vary widely in quality. This article also appeared in *Annual progress in child psychiatry and child development* (New York: Brunner/Mazel, 1988, p. 145-61).

374 **A Bermuda trail blazer: the legendary Marjorie Louise Bean.**
Nellie Eileen Musson. Hamilton, Bermuda: Business and Professional Women's Association of Bermuda, 1986. 320p. bibliog.

Bean, born in 1907, has been an educator, a champion of women's rights, a leader in charitable and cultural concerns, and a politician who has done much to change black/white relations within the Bermuda social climate. She is also a woman of 'firsts' having been appointed the first black Supervisor of Schools in 1949, the first black President of the Bermuda Society of Arts, and the first female member of the Legislative Council, both in 1980. Musson's tribute to Bean is based on interviews and both published and unpublished sources.

375 **The final report of the Royal Commission Into the Use and Misuse of Illicit Drugs and Alcohol.**
Royal Commission Into the Use and Misuse of Illicit Drugs and Alcohol. Hamilton, Bermuda: The Commission, 1985. 60p.

The Royal Commission, which was appointed and began its work in June 1983, was charged with determining the nature and extent of the use and misuse of drugs and alcohol in Bermuda. The Commission examined community participation in dealing with the drug and alcohol problem; ways to cope with the supply and demand of illicit drugs; ways to improve existing prevention, education and treatment programmes; law enforcement programmes; and the personal, social and economic costs of the misuse of drugs and alcohol. The report contains summaries and recommendations of five special reports written as part of the Commission's work.

376 **Black families in modern Bermuda: an analysis of matrifocality.**
Max Paul. Gottingen, Germany: Herodot, 1983. 122p. map. bibliog. (Monographica, no. 1).

In this revised version of his doctoral thesis, Paul focuses on the structure and function of matrifocality and links it with the socio-economic and political role of women. He examines matrifocality within several contexts: the socio-cultural process of adaptation and resistance of blacks under slavery to the economic development of Bermuda in a post-slavery period; courtship and marriage in a black socio-cultural context; the relation of courtship to illegitimacy; and the nuclear family, marriage and value systems.

377 **Blacks in Bermuda.**
Edited by W. Michael Brooke. Hamilton, Bermuda: Bermuda College, 1980. 82p.

The eleven lectures in this collection were delivered as part of Bermuda College's Extension Programme. Topics include: the origins of blacks in Bermuda; slavery in Bermuda; trades and crafts; black clubs; women and family life; education; business and the professions; religion; politics; racial characteristics and fertility patterns; and the arts (with special reference to Gombey, a traditional parade). All of the authors are recognized authorities and have written extensively in their respective fields.

378 **Mind the onion seed: black 'roots' Bermuda.**
Nellie Eileen Musson. Nashville, Tennessee: Parthenon Press, 1979. 330p.

Musson chronicles the contributions made by black women to Bermuda's growth and well-being. Covering the period from slavery to the 1970s, she emphasizes the qualities, values, desires and ambitions exhibited by these women. This fascinating contribution to Bermudian social history is well illustrated with black-and-white photographs. However, it could be improved with some editing, as well as the inclusion of an index.

379 **Bermuda and the search for blackness.**
Eva Naomi Hodgson. In: *Is massa day dead?: Black moods in the Caribbean.* Edited by Orde Coombs. Garden City, New York: Anchor Books, 1974, p. 143-64.

Hodgson discusses growing up black in a white-dominated society. She examines the activities of three Black Power movements in Bermuda: the formation of the Progressive Labour Party; a boycott of cinemas; and a labour union strike. Hodgson concludes that the Progressive Labour Party must gain political victory in order to instill self-esteem in the black population and that black Bermudians must admit to their own 'white syndrome' and begin to value themselves.

380 **Entertainment and black identity in Bermuda.**
Frank E. Manning. In: *Social and cultural identity: problems of persistence and change.* Edited by Thomas K. Fitzgerald. Athens, Georgia: Southern Anthropological Society, 1974, p. 39-50. (Southern Anthropological Society Proceedings, no. 8).

Manning's purpose is to 'deal with the symbolization of racial-cultural identity within the context of entertainment productions sponsored on a regular basis by fourteen black sports and recreational clubs licensed to serve liquor' (p. 39). The productions he considers include stage shows, dances, talent and beauty competitions, parties, fashion shows, fairs and festivals. In conjunction with these, he examines both the racial-cultural symbols of music, clothing and jewellery, and the tone symbols of elegance, sexuality and exuberance. Manning concludes that entertainment productions help to forge meaningful associations between the two sets of symbols, and are an appropriate and effective medium to convey black identity.

381 **Black clubs in Bermuda: ethnography of a play world.**
Frank E. Manning. Ithaca, New York: Cornell University Press, 1973. 277p. map. bibliog. (Symbol, Myth and Ritual Series).

This examination of the relationship between play and thought is one of the most important studies of the working class in Bermuda. The black clubs of Bermuda, which exist for the purpose of recreation, are a good setting for a study of play and an examination of thought as a social process. Manning examines the history and social aspects of the clubs as well as the economic, political and socio-cultural conditions in Bermuda.

382 **Criminal trends in Bermuda.**
Thomas M. Sheehan. *RCMP Quarterly*, vol. 32, no. 1 (July 1966), p. 21-27.

Sheehan uses crime statistics from the early 1960s to chart the trends they indicate. He concludes that there is an uncomfortably high crime rate (sixty-five per cent) among adolescent age groups, that there has been a steady increase in property crime, and that the increase in violent crimes mirrors Bermuda's economic and demographic growth.

383 **Freemasonry in Bermuda.**
Harold V. B. Voorhis. New York: The American Lodge of Research, Free and Accepted Masons, 1962. 23p.

This detailed history of Freemasonry in Bermuda from 1744 to 1962 also contains lists of Bermuda Masonic lodges and Masonic bodies, Provincial Grand Masters under England (1744-1817) and Scotland (1803-87), Grand Inspectors under England (1928-58) and Ireland (1944-54), Grand Superintendents under Scotland (1946-62), and active Masonic bodies in Bermuda in 1961.

384 **Freemasonry in Bermuda.**
A. J. B. Milborne. *Transactions of the Quatuor Coronati Lodge*, vol. 74 (1961), p. 11-31.

Milborne provides the histories of individual lodges in Bermuda: Union Lodge #266 (est. 1761), Bermuda Lodge #507 (est. 1792), Atlantic Phoenix Lodge #224 (est. 1796), St. George's Lodge #200 (est. 1797), Somerset Lodge #324 (est. 1802), Loyalty Lodge #358 (est. 1817) and St. George's Lodge #220 (est. 1856). The article includes the discussion which took place following the delivery of the paper to the Quatuor Coronati Lodge on 6 January 1961.

Health

385　Care: 100 years of hospital care in Bermuda.

J. Randolf Williams.　Hamilton, Bermuda: Camden Editions, 1994.
605p. bibliog.

A massive, detailed history of the King Edward VII Memorial Hospital in Bermuda,
based on interviews as well as documentary records. The hospital was founded in
1894 by Dr Eldon Harvey as the eight-bed Cottage Hospital. The King Edward VII
Memorial Hospital opened in 1920. This history also includes material on the Cottage
Hospital Nursing Home.

386　Heroines of the medical field of Bermuda.

Ira Philip.　Warwick, Bermuda: The Writers' Machine, 1994. 61p.
(Jacks Series, no. 2).

A good base for further research in the field, which highlights the lives and work of
five women: Elizabeth Jane Lusher, a mid-19th-century nurse; Nurse Cordelia Fubler
(1860-1957); pharmacist, Dr Olivia Tucker (1897-1995); Nurse Alice Scott (1887-?);
and Dr Kathyann L. White (1956-92).

387　Utilization of health and social services in Bermuda.

Neena L. Chappell.　*International Journal of Health Sciences*, vol. 3,
no. 2 (1992), p. 91-103.

Bermuda has no universal health insurance programme for physician and hospital
services for those aged over sixty-five. The only hospital insurance is controlled by the
government and is required by law for everyone who is working. Chappell examines
the use of physician and health care services by uninsured Bermudians and compares
these rates with those of other developed countries. Her results are based on a study of
500 uninsured Bermudians aged sixty-five and over.

388 **The legend of St. Brendans: a historical focus on mental illness in Bermuda from discovery to 1987.**
Juanita Esther Furbert Guishard.   Hamilton, Bermuda: Published by the Author, 1988. 104p.

Guishard explores the early history of mental illness in Bermuda from the witches and charmers of the 17th century, through to the lunatic asylums of the 19th century. She traces the important events and changes in attitude over several hundred years, and highlights those individuals who have made significant contributions. St. Brendans is the psychiatric hospital in Bermuda.

Politics and Government

389 The people of Bermuda: beyond the crossroads.
Barbara Harries Hunter.   Toronto: Gagne-Best, 1993. 416p. bibliog.
Hunter examines racial developments in Bermuda since 1950 and compares them with those of other bi-racial communities. She reviews political and constitutional progress and documents strikes and social unrest. Hunter also investigates developments in education, sports and the arts, focusing on many of the individuals who have been involved in these areas. This is a very detailed work, based on official sources, newspaper reports, personal recollections and interviews. An appendix lists the results of all general elections from March 1953 to February 1989.

390 Bermuda civics.
Bermuda. Ministry of Education.   Hamilton, Bermuda: The Ministry, 1992. 84p.
Produced to help students develop an interest in Bermuda and to help them better understand how the island functions, this well-laid out publication is very useful. Contents include the rights and responsibilities of the citizen and the community, communications and transport, politics, law and law making, the administration of justice, and the economy.

391 Race and party politics in Bermuda.
C. Walton Brown. *Journal of Commonwealth and Comparative Politics*, vol. 27, no. 1 (March 1989), p. 103-26.
This article is an attempt to explain the repeated electoral defeat of the Progressive Labour Party (PLP), the consistent victory of the United Bermuda Party (UBP), and the continued significance of race to the political parties of Bermuda. Brown examines the value of the non-Bermudian vote, the PLP's socialist ideology and the role of racial issues in elections. The study covers the period from 1963 to 1988.

392 **Peaceful warrior, Sir Edward Trenton Richards.**
J. Randolf Williams. Hamilton, Bermuda: Camden Editions, 1988.
375p. bibliog.

This exhaustive biography describes the life of Sir Edward Richards who was born in British Guiana in 1908 and arrived in Bermuda in 1930. He became a lawyer and then a politician, being first elected to the House of Assembly in 1948. He remained in politics, becoming Bermuda's first Premier in 1971 until his retirement in 1976, although he continued to practice law until 1986. Richards lived through a time of change and turmoil, a time of modernization of social policies and changes in racial practices. He is seen by some Bermudians as being largely responsible for the peaceful achievement of desegregation. This volume is based on newspaper stories and editorials, parliamentary debates and committee reports, speeches, reminiscences and interviews with Sir Edward.

393 **Woppened.**
Peter Woolcock. Hamilton, Bermuda: Aardvark Advertising, 1988- .
annual.

Woolcock's editorial cartoons, which provide commentary on Bermudian society, appear weekly in *The Royal Gazette* (see item no. 522). This annual is a compilation of the previous year's cartoons. 'Woppened' is Bermudian slang for 'what happened'.

394 **Bermuda: the failure of decolonisation?**
John Connell. Leeds, England: School of Geography, University of Leeds, 1987. 49p. (Working Paper 492).

Connell 'examines recent political changes in Bermuda to consider the extent to which the present political status can be conceived as a "failure" of decolonisation' (p. 1). He describes Bermuda as an artificial society, a wealthy colony which chooses to retain colonial status and which views imposed independence as a threat. Connell concludes that 'decolonisation has not failed, it has not yet been sought' (p. 41).

395 **Dr. E. F. Gordon – hero of Bermuda's working class: the political career of Dr. E. F. Gordon and the evolution of the Bermuda Workers' Association.**
Dale Butler. Warwick, Bermuda: Published by the Author, 1987.
226p.

Edgar Fitzgerald Gordon (1895-1955) was born in Trinidad and arrived in Bermuda in 1925. He was a physician, politician, labour leader and organizer who worked to change the rigid Bermuda social codes which were based on colour. He was a member of the House of Assembly, President of the Bermuda Workers' Association and President of the Bermuda Industrial Union. Butler outlines the role Dr Gordon played during an important period of social reconstruction in Bermuda.

396 **Freedom fighters: from Monk to Mazumbo.**
Ira Philip. London: Akira Press, 1987. 275p.

Philip outlines the struggle of Bermudian workers for civil rights and political equality in the first half of the 20th century. He emphasizes the work of two men: the American clergyman and journalist, Charles Vinton Monk; and the West Indian surgeon, Edgar

Fitzgerald Gordon, who was also known as Mazumbo. The book profiles the struggles of the time and describes the island's politics and politicians.

397 Man of stature: Sir Henry James Tucker.
J. Randolf Williams. Hamilton, Bermuda: Camden Editions, 1987. 269p. bibliog.

Sir Henry Tucker (1903-86) was 'one of the most important figures in Bermuda's history, and his influence will be felt for many years to come' (p. xii). An important member of Bermuda's banking industry and government, he became Secretary to the Bank of Bermuda in 1934 and Manager in 1938 until his retirement in 1969. Tucker was a member of the House of Assembly from 1938 to 1948 and 1953 to 1971 and in 1964 was elected leader of the United Bermuda Party. This biography, an important record of Bermuda in the 20th century, is based on personal interviews, newspaper accounts, parliamentary records and private papers.

398 Campaign rhetoric in Bermuda: the politics of race and religion.
Frank E. Manning. In: *Politically speaking: cross-cultural studies of rhetoric*. Edited by Robert Paine. Philadelphia: Institute for the Study of Human Issues, 1981, p. 165-84.

Examines the campaign rhetoric of black Bermudians. In particular, Manning looks at its relationship to their ideology, its role in defining their cultural and political opposition to whites, and its effectiveness in winning intellectual agreement and electoral support.

399 Race and democracy in Bermuda: the fight for the right.
Frank E. Manning. *Caribbean Review*, vol. 10, no. 2 (Spring 1981), p. 20-23.

In the December 1980 general election both Bermuda political parties moved closer to the right in their approach to the voters. The United Bermuda Party, which won the election, campaigned as custodians of the economy, advocating capitalism with a social conscience. The Progressive Labour Party saw itself as a proponent of capitalism with a black face. Manning discusses Bermuda's voting culture and patterns. He also comments on possible independence and a political or quasi-political relationship with Canada.

400 Religion and politics in Bermuda: revivalist politics and the language of power.
Frank E. Manning. *Caribbean Review*, vol. 8, no. 4 (Fall 1979), p. 18-21, 42-43.

Manning discusses the link between evangelical, revivalist language and politics in the 1976 election campaign. The Progressive Labour Party replaced Black Power rhetoric with evangelism. Party members saw themselves as crusaders against evil and campaign rallies resembled religious services. Manning suggests that the use of massed church choirs and pastors as rally speakers, along with Old Testament imagery, linked religion and politics in the minds of the black voters.

401 **Bermudian politics in transition: race, voting, and public opinion.**
Frank E. Manning. Hamilton, Bermuda: Island Press, 1978. 231p.
bibliog.

This detailed analysis of contemporary political thought and action is primarily based
on two surveys taken after the 1976 election. Manning discusses both the Bermudian
political process and the issues and sentiments of the electorate at the time of the
election. His most fascinating find is the pivotal role played by black women in the
Progressive Labour Party's success. Appendices provide copies of the surveys and
commentary on the statistical significance of the findings.

402 **Plutocracy v. democracy: a political perspective.**
Eugene Stovell, edited by Dale Butler. Southampton, Bermuda:
Bermuda for Bermudians, 1978. 40p.

This collection of editorial cartoons, which Stovell began drawing for *The Workers
Voice* in 1975, highlights political and social problems such as unemployment, the
voting process, anti-colonialism and property ownership. The cartoons are not dated.

403 **The big brother: Canadian cultural symbolism and Bermudian
political thought.**
Frank E. Manning. *Revista/Review Interamericana*, vol. 7, no. 1
(Spring 1977), p. 60-72.

This article focuses on the presence in Bermuda of Canadian religious, educational
and prestige/authority symbols, and the emergence in Bermuda of support for a future
political relationship with Canada. Manning details the influence of several Canadian
religious denominations (the Anglican Church, the Roman Catholic Church and the
Methodist Church) and educational institutions (Mount Allison University and Ridley
College). He points out that Bermuda College has been modelled on Canadian
community colleges and that a number of Canadians have held positions of prestige
and authority throughout Bermuda's history. Manning concludes by examining the
political debate between independence from Great Britain and political affiliation with
Canada that emerged in the 1970s.

404 **Politics in an artificial society.**
Selwyn D. Ryan. *Caribbean Studies*, vol. 15, no. 2 (July 1975),
p. 5-35.

Examines the impact of race, history and tourism on the political and social life of
Bermuda. There are sections on society, politics, the Progressive Labour Party, the
United Bermuda Party, the Black Beret Cadre (Bermuda's equivalent to the Black
Panther Party) and a number of contemporary issues including education, immigra-
tion, job opportunities, drugs and alcoholism. This article also appeared in *Ethnicity in
the Americas*, edited by Frances Henry (The Hague: Mouton, 1976, p. 159-92).

405 **Colonel Tom Dill O. B. E.: lawyer, soldier & statesman.**
Lloyd Mayer. Hamilton, Bermuda: Bermuda Book Stores, 1964. 197p.

Thomas Melville Dill (1876-1945) was a prominent lawyer, soldier and politician.
This biographical study provides information on Dill and his influential family, as
well as a social history of Bermuda during his lifetime. There is no index.

406 **And now Bermuda.**
E. La Mothe Stowell. *The National Review*, vol. 129 (1947),
p. 298-305.

Stowell discusses a petition sent to the Colonial Office in London in November 1946 by the Bermuda Workers' Association, requesting a Royal Commission to investigate economic, social and political conditions in Bermuda. Stowell suggests that the then newly elected Socialist government in Great Britain was not experienced enough to handle the situation. This article provides an interesting glimpse of postwar Bermuda politics and social conditions.

Constitution and Legal System

Constitution

407   The constitution of Bermuda.
Bermuda.   Hamilton, Bermuda: Bermuda Press, 1981. 90p.

This is the Bermuda Constitution Order of 1968 which outlines the rights and responsibilities of the people and government of Bermuda. There are sections on the protection of fundamental rights and freedoms of the individual; the responsibilities of the governor, the legislature, the executive and the judiciary; the role of the public service; and finance.

408   Bermuda constitutional documents.
Compiled by William M. Cox.   Hamilton, Bermuda: Published by the Author, 1970. 120p.

Cox has brought together transcriptions of Bermuda's most important constitutional documents including: the Commission of Richard Moore (1612); the Articles of the First Settlers (1612); The Charter of the Bermuda Company (1615); the Account of the First Assembly of the Bermuda Parliament (1620); the Dissolution of the Bermuda Company (1684); the Emancipation Act (1834); and the Bermuda Constitution (1968). There is also a list of Bermuda governors from 1612 to 1964. Cox compiled this work to celebrate the 350th anniversary of the Bermuda Parliament.

409   Report of the Bermuda Constitutional Conference 1966.
London: HMSO, 1967. 23p. (Cmnd. 3174).

This document reports on constitutional meetings held in London in November 1966. It also includes several appendices: a summary of provisions for a new constitution; the minority report written by two independent members of the Bermuda House of Assembly; the minority report written by the representatives of Bermuda's Progressive Labour Party; and a list of those attending the conference.

410   **On the constitutional history of the Bermudas, the oldest remaining British plantation.**
John Henry Lefroy. *Archaeologia*, vol. 47 (1883), p. 65-82.
Lefroy, Governor of Bermuda from 1871 to 1877, presents a detailed examination of the development of constitutional government in Bermuda from the early 17th century to the late 18th century. He also describes the duties of the House of Assembly and its officials and its members.

Legal system

411   **Bermuda Consolidated Index of Statutes and Subsidiary Legislation to . . .**
Faculty of Law Library. University of the West Indies. Barbados.
Cave Hill, Barbados: Faculty of Law Library, 1986- . annual.
One of a series in the West Indian Legislation Indexing Project (WILIP), produced in co-operation with the British Development Division.

412   **Bermuda's crime and punishment 17th century style.**
Terry Tucker.   Hamilton, Bermuda: Island Press, 1973. 36p.
This fascinating booklet outlines the laws in place and the punishments exacted for crimes committed in 17th-century Bermuda. Tucker provides examples of crimes and the punishments given for those particular crimes. She also explains such punishments as the ducking stool and stocks; branding and whipping; imprisonment and banishment; and the treadmill. Tucker attempts to place crime and punishment in the context of the time, giving a description of the social conditions which prevailed and the nature of the legal system which sought to impose law and order.

413   **Public acts of the Legislature of the Islands of Bermuda together with statutory instruments in force thereunder, revised and compiled under the authority of the Revised Laws and Annual Revision Act, 1971, by the Attorney-General of Bermuda.**
Hamilton, Bermuda: Government of Bermuda; London: Sweet and Maxwell, 1971- . 7 vols.
This is the eighth compilation of the revised laws of Bermuda since the first collection in 1862. This current compilation is in loose-leaf format and is constantly updated.

Economy

414 **The economic consequences of political independence: the case of Bermuda.**
James C. W. Ahiakpor.   Vancouver, British Columbia, Canada: The Fraser Institute, 1990. 76p. bibliog.

Ahiakpor finds that most Bermudians do not actively seek independence from Great Britain. They have virtually total control over all facets of their lives except external representation and national security. He examines both sides of the issue and concludes that political independence would not ruin Bermuda's potential for continued economic success and that the costs of independence are not beyond the country's means. However, he also concludes that the benefits do not seem to be worth the cost.

415 **Bermuda: an Economic Review.**
Bermuda. Ministry of Finance.   Hamilton, Bermuda: The Ministry, 1983- . annual.

Includes a number of tables and charts, and provides discussion on such topics as gross domestic product, employment and incomes, financial conditions and balance of payments.

Finance and Business

416 The 1994 guide to offshore financial centres.
London: Euromoney Publications, 1994. 82p.

The 'Bermuda' section (p. 23-29) contains background material on the establishment of the island as an offshore financial centre in the 1930s and its dramatic growth in the 1960s (by 1993, for example, there were more than 7,500 international businesses registered). There is also information on the regulatory environment, insurance companies, fund management, shipping and the country's fiscal framework.

417 Don't sell Bermuda short.
David Fairlamb. *Institutional Investor: International Edition*, vol. 18, no. 8 (Aug. 1993), p. 57-62.

Fairlamb provides background financial information, discusses Bermuda's liberal regulatory environment and examines the country's slowed financial growth. More importantly, he highlights Bermuda's advantages: accessibility, political stability, an excellent infrastructure and a congenial lifestyle. There is particular emphasis on the insurance industry. There is also a sidebar (p. 60-61), entitled 'Trade winds of change at the BSE', which examines the Bermuda Stock Exchange.

418 Household expenditure survey 1993.
Bermuda. Ministry of Finance. Statistics Department. Hamilton, Bermuda: The Ministry, 1993. 41p.

The aim of this survey is 'to obtain expenditure data from private households and analyze the data with respect to the socioeconomic structure of households in Bermuda' (p. 1). The survey, based on questionnaires and door-to-door canvassing, includes information on both expenditures and incomes, and contains thirteen tables of statistics.

419　**First, one thousand miles . . . : Bermudian enterprise and the Bank of Bermuda.**
Gordon Phillips.　Hamilton, Bermuda: The Bank of Bermuda, 1992. 242p. bibliog.

A well-illustrated history of both the Bank of Bermuda, established in 1889, and Bermudian finance and business. The appendices list the bank's presidents and chairmen, vice presidents and deputy chairmen, officers and directors from 1889 onwards.

420　**Pleasures of the Caribbean.**
Jonathan Burton.　*Far Eastern Economic Review*, vol. 155, no. 9 (5 March 1992), p. 42-43.

Burton compares the offshore advantages of the Bahamas, Bermuda, the British Virgin Islands, the Cayman Islands, Nevis, Panama, and the Turks and Caicos Islands. Bermuda tends to scrutinize its newcomers more carefully, and is the favoured domicile among offshore unit trust managers, financial services and insurance companies.

421　**Doing business in Bermuda.**
Price Waterhouse.　Hamilton, Bermuda: Price Waterhouse, 1991. 82p.

This booklet was previously published in 1975 and 1985. The current edition contains information on the business environment, foreign investment and trade opportunities, investment incentives, restrictions on foreign investment and investors, the regulatory environment, banking and finance, exporting, labour relations and working conditions, audit requirements and practices, accounting principles and practices, and the tax system. There is also a general profile of the country.

422　**Doing business in Bermuda.**
Ernst & Young.　Hamilton, Bermuda: Ernst & Young, 1990. 40p.

This booklet, similar to Price Waterhouse's *Doing business in Bermuda* (see preceding entry), provides information on forms of business organization, insurance companies, accounting and auditing, and taxation. There is also a general profile of the country.

423　**Butterfield's Bank: five generations in Bermuda.**
Harry Chester Butterfield.　Hamilton, Bermuda: Bermuda Book Stores, 1958. 112p. map.

A history of the prominent Bermuda bank, published to mark its centenary. The Bank of N. T. Butterfield was established in 1858 by Nathaniel Butterfield (1788-1868). This book provides information on the bank itself as well as on Bermuda's economic development over the same one hundred years. Appendices include a list of depositors in 1884, a list of bank presidents from 1904 to 1958, and lists of the bank directors and bank officers for 1958.

Industry, Trade and Labour

424 **The Bermuda fisheries: a tragedy of the commons averted?**
James N. Butler, James Burnett-Herkes, John A. Barnes.
Environment, vol. 35, no. 1 (Jan./Feb. 1993), p. 6-15, 25-27, 29-33.
The authors discuss the decline in the numbers of grouper and the increase in the catch of herbivorous reef fish over a two decade period which led, by the 1980s, to a concern regarding the exhausted desirable fish stocks and the changing integrity of the reef community. The article contains fisheries statistics, a description of the fisheries industry, comments on fisheries regulations, and a discussion of the government's role in the industry. There are also descriptions of the fish which make up the industry, a discussion of reef ecology, and an outline of alternative fishing methods.

425 **'The fish pot ban': reef overfishing and state management in Bermuda.**
Gene Barrett. *Maritime Anthropological Studies*, vol. 4, no. 2 (1991), p. 17-39.
Barrett examines the problem of commercial overfishing in a subtropical reef fishery, the failure of management to intercede, and the prospects for fishery co-management. He explains that the overfishing was a result of a number of economic developments and state regulatory measures. The use of fish pots was banned in 1990 in an attempt to rehabilitate the reef fishery which accounted for two-thirds of the total food fish landings and three-quarters of the fishermen's income. Barrett concludes that the ban on pot fishing will not solve the industry's problems and that co-management solutions need to be sought.

426 **Assessment of the potential for aquaculture in Bermuda.**
Edited by Thomas D. Sleeter. St. George, Bermuda: Bermuda
Biological Station for Research, 1984. 191p. (Special Publication,
no. 27).

These proceedings of workshops held in Bermuda, 11-15 October 1983, conclude that
resource assessment is necessary to identify potential species and their habitats, and
develop appropriate government policies, while economic assessment is necessary to
identify a market and establish economic incentives. The seventeen papers cover the
topics of economic and legislative perspectives; bivalve fish culture; and the culture of
other potential species.

427 **Bermudian handline fishing in the sailing sloop era: a fisherman's
account.**
Raoul Andersen. In: *The fishing culture of the world: studies in
ethnology, cultural ecology and folklore.* Edited by Bela Gunda.
Budapest: Akademiai Kiado, 1984, p. 777-801.

Andersen's study of the relatively isolated Bermudian fishing industry is based on a
two-week visit in January 1975. His contribution to this volume is primarily a
personal account of Captain Geary Pitcher, Sr., a retired St. David's Island commercial fisherman. The article includes a glossary of St. David's Island sloop fishing
technology and nineteen black-and-white photographs.

428 **Thank you, Dr. E. F. Gordon.**
Gerald Alexander Brangman. New York: Vantage Press, 1973. 60p.

Brangman, who was briefly the first president of The Bermuda Workers' Union
(renamed The Bermuda Workers' Association) and the first vice president of The
Bermuda Industrial Union, provides a personal account of the birth of the labour
movement in Bermuda in the 1940s under the leadership of Dr Edgar Fitzgerald
Gordon. This work contains the full text of a petition sent to the British Secretary of
State for the Colonies in 1946 requesting a Royal Commission to investigate labour
practices and social, economic and political conditions in Bermuda. The Secretary's
reply and the response of the Governor of Bermuda are also included.

429 **A short history of whaling in Bermuda.**
Edward F. Schortman. *The Mariner's Mirror*, vol. 55, no. 1
(Feb. 1969), p. 77-85.

The discovery of ambergris in 1611 marked the beginning of the Bermuda whaling
industry which started to decline by the end of the 18th century and continued on a
small scale until the 1880s. Schortman outlines the industry's history, describing its
various components and the government's involvement over time.

430   **Trade and commerce of Bermuda, 1515-1839, and old sea captains' tales.**
Mary Alicia Juliette Arton.   Hamilton, Bermuda: Island Press, 1965.
256p. map.

This comprehensive history of sea trade and commerce is based on the author's 'ten exercise books, all meticulously written in long hand. . . . [T]here have been no deletions or addendums. . . . ' (Introduction). The work includes material from official sources and quotations from contemporary documents. There are also lists of individuals and vessels prominent in the sea trade. Arton includes a chapter on the salt trade connection between the Turk's Island and Bermuda.

Communications

431   **A century of progress: a history of the Bermuda Telephone Company Ltd., 1887-1987.**
Colin H. Benbow.   Hamilton, Bermuda: Bermuda Telephone Co., 1987. 133p.
A detailed history written to celebrate the first 100 years of the company's existence. Benbow has based his research on original documents and company records.

Transport

432 The Bermuda Railway: gone but not forgotten.

Colin A. Pomeroy.   Devon, Bermuda: Published by the Author, 1993.
117p. 4 maps. bibliog.

The Bermuda Railway was formally opened in 1931 and closed in 1948. Pomeroy
emphasizes the railway's technical history in this well-illustrated book, and also
describes the Railway Trail, opened in 1984, which allows walkers to follow the old
railway bed throughout the island. Appendices include information on the original
rolling stock, stations, bridges, trestles, tunnels and level crossings.

433 'Rattle and Shake': the story of the Bermuda Railway.

David F. Raine.   St. George, Bermuda: Pompano Publications, 1992.
93p. 2 maps.

Traces the history of the Bermuda Railway from the first discussions on its construction in 1893 to its demise in the late 1940s. Raine outlines its development, the
financial woes encountered, its social impact and the reasons why it was dismantled
and sold to British Guiana (now Guyana). There are forty-five excellent black-and-
white photographs, including a selection showing the Railway Trail segments which
can be walked today. An appendix provides details of relevant acts and legislation.

434 A streetcar few desired: the Bermuda Trolley Company, 1910-11.

Duncan McDowall.   *Business History*, vol. 27, no. 1 (March 1985),
p. 43-58.

McDowall outlines the proposal by a group of Canadian businessmen in 1910 to
construct an electric tramway system stretching from one end of Bermuda to the other.
The ensuing parliamentary debate and successful opposition centred on conservation
and economic issues. The company and the proposal were short-lived.

Postal System

435 Postal history of blockade running through Bermuda 1861-1865.
Morris Hoadley Ludington.   Ottawa: British Caribbean Philatelic
Study Group, 1996. 47p. (Monograph, no. 14).

Ludington describes how the post got from the Southern States to England via
Bermuda and vice versa during the American Civil War. He provides descriptions and
black-and-white photographs of the covers and contents of fifteen such letters. There
is also a list of blockade runners to and from Bermuda between 1861 and 1865.

436 Bermuda mails to 1865: an inventory of the postal markings.
Michel Forand, Charles Freeland.   Ottawa: British Caribbean
Philatelic Study Group, 1995. 118p. 2 maps. bibliog. (Monograph,
no. 13).

In the first section of this book, the authors outline the postal history of Bermuda to
1865. They examine the postal service, handstamps, correspondence and postal
archives. The second section comprises an inventory, recording every surviving
example of postal handstamped markings and forwarding-agents' cachets used in
Bermuda during the period from 1820 to 1882.

437 The King George V high-value stamps of Bermuda, 1917-1938.
Myles Glazer.   Marblehead, Massachusetts: Published by the Author,
1994. 208p. bibliog.

In this highly detailed examination of the Bermudian stamps issued during the reign of
George V (1910-36), Glazer discusses production and delivery; usage and distribution;
physical characteristics; colour analysis and varieties; plate flaws; and printing
identification, frequency and valuation. The work is well illustrated and includes a
glossary.

438   **Vignettes of early British North American postal history, XXII: the Bermuda connection.**
John Carstairs Arnell.   *The Canadian Philatelist*, vol. 43, no. 3 (May-June 1992), p. 200-03.

Describes Bermuda's role in communications between Britain and North America, concentrating on mail packets from 1806 to the 1820s. Three examples of letters sent by such mail packets illustrate the article.

439   **The Furness Line to Bermuda.**
Morris Hoadley Ludington, Michael R. Rego.   Ottawa: British Caribbean Philatelic Study Group, 1990. 58p. (Monograph, no. 11).

The Furness Bermuda Line ran luxury liners between New York and Bermuda and cruises out of New York from 1919 to 1966. The authors provide a history of the company but over half of this work (p. 10-41) contains illustrations of the ship markings (i.e., postal markings) of letters mailed from the ships of the Furness Bermuda Line and the Bermuda and West Indies Steamship Company, which was related to Furness. Black-and-white photographs of the liners and a selection of advertisements for the Furness Bermuda Line are included.

440   **The postal history and stamps of Bermuda.**
Morris Hoadley Ludington.   Lawrence, Massachusetts: Quarterman Publications, 1978. 432p. 6 maps. bibliog.

Section one of this very detailed volume outlines the history of the postal service from 1784 to 1948 and includes examples of and commentary on postal markings and cancellations. Section two examines the adhesive stamps from 1848 to 1949, and provides information on postal stationery. There are black-and-white photographs only.

441   **Bermuda: the post office, postal markings and adhesive stamps.**
Morris Hoadley Ludington.   London: Robson Lowe, 1962. 283p. 9 maps. bibliog.

Book one, part one outlines Bermuda postal history from 1784 to the 1940s, while book one, part two contains information on postal cancellations with accompanying illustrations. Book one, part three comprises a series of appendices of government documents pertinent to the postal system, tables of postage rates, a list of post offices and a list of postal officials. Book two contains the text related to adhesive stamps in use from 1848 to 1950. The third section, the Appendices, contains a summary of stamp printings and dates received in Bermuda from 1865 to 1941, and a check-list of stamps from 1865 to 1949. The book is well documented and well illustrated with fifty black-and-white plates of postal officials, post offices, envelopes and letters, and stamps.

442   **Bermuda: the handstruck stamps and cancellations.**
Morris Hoadley Ludington.   London: Robson Lowe, 1956. 40p. map.

This very detailed history and check-list of handstruck stamps and cancellations from the 1820s onwards also includes black-and-white photographs of three Bermudian post offices.

Numismatics

443 **A history of Bermuda and its paper money.**
Nelson Page Aspen. Devon, Pennsylvania: Wm. T. Cooke Pub. Ltd.,
1980. 120p. map.

Aspen provides descriptions and colour plates of the paper currency used in Bermuda
from the reign of George V to the late 1970s. This survey includes both sterling notes
used from 1910 to 1970 and decimal notes introduced in 1970. A useful glossary is
included.

444 **The Bank of Bermuda coin collection: coins used for trading in
Bermuda from the 16th century to the present date.**
The Bank of Bermuda. Hamilton, Bermuda: The Bank, 1979. 58p.
map. bibliog.

An account and complete catalogue of the more than 570 coins in the Bank's
collection which includes Bermudian coins up to the reign of Elizabeth II plus the
English-American colonies' coins and tokens which circulated in Bermuda well into
the 19th century. Black-and-white photographs illustrate fifty-five of the coins
described.

Environment

445 **Paradise regained: bringing an island back to life.**
J. A. Pollard. *Oceans*, vol. 18, no. 4 (July/Aug. 1985), p. 42-49.
From the 1600s to the mid-1900s many species of flora and fauna were brought to near extinction due to the ravages of humans. In 1961 David Wingate (b. 1935) became Warden of the much neglected Nonsuch Island off the coast of Bermuda. He resolved to create a 'living museum' by reintroducing native plants and animals, and began by culling everything that had not existed on Bermuda in 1609. His project proved to be a success; for example, by 1973 the cahow bird population had surpassed 100 for the first time in three centuries. A separate article, 'Applying the lessons of Nonsuch' (p. 46-47), also by Pollard, is contained within the main article.

446 **Bermuda's delicate balance: people and the environment.**
Edited by Stuart J. Hayward, Vicki Holt Gomez, Wolfgang Sterrer.
Hamilton, Bermuda: The Bermuda National Trust, 1981. 402p. 3 maps.
One of the most thorough investigations ever undertaken in Bermuda to study the delicate relationship between the people of Bermuda and their natural environment. It is a report of the impact of human activities on a closed, fragile tropical island eco-system. Thirty-four authors have produced a total of twenty-eight papers on a variety of subjects covering ecological, demographic, sociological and economic aspects.

447 **The Bermuda marine environment: a report on the Bermuda Inshore Waters Investigations 1976-1977.**
Byron Morris, John Barnes, Foster Brown, John Markham. St.
Georges West, Bermuda: Bermuda Biological Station, 1977.
120p. 23 maps. bibliog. (Special Publication, no. 15).
The report of a multidisciplinary environmental quality study of the Bermuda inshore waters. Topics discussed include geology, the human environment, morphology and morphometry, sediments, waters and organisms. There are 155 figures and 66 tables of statistics scattered throughout the text.

448   **The Bermuda Islands and the Bermuda Biological Station for Research.**
E. L. Mark.   *Proceedings of the American Association for the Advancement of Science*, vol. 54 (Dec. 1904), p. 471-501.

An excellent introduction to both the natural history of Bermuda and the beginnings of the Bermuda Biological Station for Research. In the main part of the article (p. 471-98), Mark comments on topography, geography, geology, flora and fauna, marine life, population and architecture. He also outlines previous research undertaken by Heilprin, Agassiz and Verrill. There are sixteen plates with thirty-one black-and-white illustrations following p. 501.

Statistics

449 Bermuda digest of statistics.
Bermuda. Ministry of Finance.   Hamilton, Bermuda: The Ministry,
1973- . annual.

This publication provides statistics on population, education, health, law enforcement,
labour, prices and wages, home finances, national accounts and balance of payments,
external trade, transport, international travel and weather. There is no text to support
the tables of figures. Where possible the statistics listed are for the preceding ten years
for comparison purposes.

Education

450 In pursuit of excellence, The Bermuda High School for Girls 1894-1994.
Rebecca Zuill.   Hamilton, Bermuda: Bermuda High School for Girls Association, 1995. 154p.

The Bermuda High School for Girls was established through the efforts of Mrs Grosvenor Tucker. This centenary publication, written by a former student, is based on archival sources, correspondence, previous school publications, student and teacher reminiscences, and public addresses by school personnel.

451 A school is born: a history of St. George's Grammar School Bermuda 1875-1975.
Thomas F. Davies.   St. George, Bermuda: St. George's Grammar School, 1988. 152p.

The author, a former headmaster of the school, presents a methodical, year-by-year history of the school, now known as St. George's Preparatory School. The work also includes lists of the Chairmen of the Board (1909-88), head teachers (1876-1977), members of the Board (1875-1988) and staff members from 1876 onwards.

452 The Berkeley Educational Society's origins and early history.
Kenneth Ellsworth Robinson.   Pembroke, Bermuda: Berkeley Educational Society, 1962. 88p.

Provides the history of the formation and work of the Berkeley Educational Society from its foundation in 1879 to the opening of the Institute in 1897. The Berkeley Educational Society heralded the beginning of higher education on a non-segregated basis in Bermuda. The Institute came to serve mainly the black community and, as such, many of the black leaders in contemporary Bermuda are listed among its graduates. Robinson's treatise outlines the original constitution and the early campaigns for support waged by the Society's founders. He has included excerpts from early documents and black-and-white photographs of the early members. Appendices include the Devonshire College Act (1870), the Berkeley Educational Society Act (1882), and the Society's Constitution (1882). Robinson was curator-historian of the Society.

Language and Dialects

453 Bermewjan vurds: a dictionary of conversational Bermudian.
Compiled and edited by Peter A. Smith, Fred M. Barritt.   Hamilton, Bermuda: Island Press, 1984. 56p.

The compilers have gathered together a collection of distinctly Bermudian idioms and slang, omitting those terms which may be used in Bermuda but are not uniquely Bermudian. They also comment on the Bermudian pronunciation of the letter 'v' as a 'w' (and vice versa) and the frequent pronunciation of the letter 'e' as 'a'.

454 Bermudian English.
Harry Morgan Ayres. *American Speech*, vol. 8, no. 1 (Feb. 1933), p. 3-10.

In this analysis of the Bermudian dialect, Ayres traces some of the peculiarities of pronunciation and vernacular spelling back to their origins in Britain and the United States. He pays particular attention to the transposition/interchange of 'v's and 'w's which was common as early as the late 18th century.

Literature

Anthologies

455 An isle so long unknown: short stories.
Bermuda Writers' Collective, edited by Angela Barry, Rawle
Frederick, Ronald Lightbourne, Nelda Simons.   Devonshire,
Bermuda: The Collective, 1993. 212p.

This collection of thirteen short stories by thirteen published and unpublished authors
is similar to the Collective's first publication, *Palmetto wine (short stories)* (see item
no. 457).

456 Mirror of our souls.
Inspirational Writers Association.   Pembroke, Bermuda: The
Association, 1990. 164p.

In this, its first major project, the Inspirational Writers Association attempts to draw
some of its novice poets out into the public view. The collection of 117 poems is
organized into five sections: 'Visions of Truth', 'Island Thoughts', 'Words of
Wisdom', 'Echoes of Love', and 'Native Flames'. The works of fourteen poets are
presented in this anthology but four of the poets in particular are featured: Alice K.
Binns, Joy Wilson-Tucker, C. Waverley Minors and Shirley D. Rogers.

457 Palmetto wine (short stories).
Bermuda Writers' Collective.   Devonshire, Bermuda: The Collective,
1990. 149p.

The Bermuda Writers' Collective's first publication is a collection of fourteen short
stories by nine published and unpublished authors.

458   Longtales: a Bermuda Writers Club anthology.
Edited by Ira Philip.   Hamilton, Bermuda: Bermuda Writers Club and
Bermuda Arts Council, 1982. 96p.
A collection of thirty poems, thirteen prose pieces and one song with music.

Children's literature

459   Tiny goes back in time: a Bermuda history tour.
Elizabeth A. Mulderig.   Hamilton, Bermuda: Bermudian Pub. Co.,
1994. 40p.
Tiny the tree frog dreams that he goes back in time to the early 1600s to the wreck of
the *Sea Venture*. He also dreams of whaling and fishing, of being subjected to the
ducking stool and the stocks, and of consorting with pirates. Delightful rhyming text
and bright paintings enliven the third of this series of children's picture books.

460   Tiny tours Bermuda's ocean.
Elizabeth A. Mulderig.   Hamilton, Bermuda: Bermudian Pub. Co.,
1993. 40p.
In the second book of the series, Tiny the tree frog meets strange fish, shy plants, a
haunted shipwreck, turtles with no table manners, and other salt water creatures.

461   Tiny the tree frog tours Bermuda.
Elizabeth A. Mulderig.   Hamilton, Bermuda: Bermudian Pub. Co.,
1992. 40p.
In the first of the series, Tiny rides on the back of a horse and buggy to tour Bermuda.
He visits old forts and churches, sandy beaches, the city of Hamilton, craft shops and
the Dockyard.

Individual authors

462   Bermuda folklore and calypso poems.
Stanley Seymour.   London: Avon Books, 1995. 119p.
The eighty-nine poems in this collection were written to commemorate events and
people, or to highlight legends and folklore tales. Each poem is introduced with an
annotation or background information. Seymour is one of Bermuda's leading
calypsonians.

463 **Battle for freedom: Bermudian drama and poetry.**
Shangri-La Durham-Thompson. Hamilton, Bermuda: The Writers'
Machine, 1994. 320p.

A collection of twelve plays (five one-acts, six two-acts, one three-act), three puppet
plays and twenty poems by Durham-Thompson. 'The plays espouse the cause of black
Bermudians through their everyday lives in accent and idiom' (Foreword, p. xiii).

464 **The vendor of dreams & other stories.**
Rawle Frederick. Devonshire, Bermuda: Bermuda Writers'
Collective, 1992. 119p.

These seven short stories were written by the Trinidadian-born Frederick. In his
introduction, Cyril Packwood describes Frederick's work: 'With economy of expression
and a fine eye for detail, the author has crafted well-written and thought provoking
short stories' (p. 11).

465 **Queen of the east: an heroic story of Bermuda's one-time brothel
and other stories.**
John Weatherill. Kilmington, England: Morrell Wylye Head, 1988.
92p.

These nine tales of mystery are set in Bermuda and based on historical fact.

466 **The St. Georges dream: a collection of short stories and vignettes.**
Sandra Taylor Rouja. Hamilton, Bermuda: Island Press, 1988. 94p.

These short stories and prose pieces are taken from the author's journals which she
kept while living in France (1977-80) and Bermuda (1970-76, 1981-84). Many of the
pieces reflect Rouja's Portuguese heritage in a Bermudian context.

467 **A few flowers for St. George.**
Brian Burland. New York: Norton, 1986. 256p.

Continues the story of James Berkeley, the hero of Burland's *A fall from aloft* (see
item no. 470), who is now twenty years old, and who searches for love and truth in
this full and detailed family saga. Burland explores homelessness and deep longing in
the 20th century, and studies the post-Freudian visitation of the sins of one generation
onto the next. The St. George of the title refers to James Berkeley's father. This novel
was first published in London (Barrie & Rockliff, 1969).

468 **Hang the witch high! or, the false ebony tree: a story of Bermuda
witchcraft.**
Terry Tucker. Hamilton, Bermuda: Island Press, 1977. 99p.

This novel, set in Bermuda in 1664, tells the story of sixteen-year old Gillian
Saunders, the daughter of a school master, condemned through malicious gossip as a
witch. Tucker's faithfulness to the historical and geographical background adds
realism to her tale. *Hang the witch high!* was originally published by the Bermuda
Historical Society in 1963 as its Occasional Publication, no. 5 under the title of *The
false ebony tree*.

469 **Surprise.**
Brian Burland. London: George Allen & Unwin; New York: Harper
& Row, 1974. 235p.
Set in Bermuda in the 1840s, the novel follows the life of a black Bermudian seaman,
Surprise Billinghurst, during the years after the abolition of slavery when he leaves
Bermuda to found a colony on Barbuda. This so-called rebellion is put down in seven
minutes of bombardment by HMS *Achilles* two years after the colony is established.
The novel is based on historical events and examines the social conditions and racial
relationships evident at the time.

470 **A fall from aloft.**
Brian Burland. London: Barrie & Rockliff; New York: Random
House, 1968. 194p.
Set in 1942, Burland's first novel depicts thirteen-year old James Berkeley's coming
of age as he is sent to Britain for schooling. This memorable story is a well-crafted,
probing study of adolescence.

471 **Rendezvous with destiny: reader's edition of a play in three acts.**
Terry Tucker. Hamilton, Bermuda: Bermuda Historical Society,
1958. 22p. (Occasional Publication, no. 1).
This historical play about the founding of Bermuda is based on archival and
government documents. It was written to commemorate the 350th anniversary of the
shipwreck of the *Sea Venture* which led to the colonization of Bermuda.

Foreign literature set in Bermuda

472 **Beast.**
Peter Benchley. London: Hutchinson; New York: Ballantine Books,
1991. 350p.
Another example of Benchley's escapist fiction with the evil in *Beast* taking the form
of a giant squid. The suspense is consistent and compelling, and the characters are
interesting and colourful.

473 **The salt rakers.**
Barbara Whitnell. London: Hodder & Stoughton, 1986. 352p.
Set in Bermuda in 1811, this is the saga of a family trying to build a life on a small
hurricane-swept island. *The salt rakers* is historically accurate and explores, among
other things, the relation between Bermuda and the Turks and Caicos Islands where,
for decades, Bermudians travelled to rake the salt which became a mainstay of their
late 18th- and early 19th-century economy.

474 **Tom Moore's Bermuda poems and notes.**
Tom Moore, with comment by William Edward Sears Zuill.
Hamilton, Bermuda: Bermuda Book Stores, 1978. 40p.

During his five-month stay in Bermuda in 1804, the Irish poet, Tom Moore (1779-1852), wrote thirteen poems, four of which are reproduced in this booklet: 'Epistle III to the Marchioness Dowager of Donegal from Bermuda, January 1804', 'Epistle IV to George Morgan, Esq. of Norfolk, Virginia from Bermuda, January 1804', 'Odes to Nea written at Bermuda' and 'Epistle V to Joseph Atkinson, Esq. from Bermuda, March 1804'. Zuill provides extensive notes and commentary.

475 **The deep.**
Peter Benchley. London: André Deutsch; Garden City, New York: Doubleday, 1976. 252p.

A honeymoon couple diving off Bermuda find ampoules of morphine from a Second World War shipwreck. This discovery attracts underworld figures who, along with a vicious moray eel, provide the suspense and adventure. As well as being good escapist fiction, *The deep* contains a wealth of casual information on Bermudian history, sociology, climate, flora and fauna, skin diving and treasure hunting.

476 **Paradiso.**
Allan Prior. London: Cassell; New York: Simon & Schuster, 1972. 320p.

Prior's story pits the New York entertainment industry against local politics in Bermuda.

477 **The Sea 'Venture.**
F. Van Wyck Mason. Garden City, New York: Doubleday, 1961. 349p.

A fictional account of the wreck of the *Sea Venture* off the coast of Bermuda in 1609. The author has based his novel on thorough historic research with a minimum of contrived incident and a minimum of fictional characters. He explains that the apostrophe appears in the title because research shows that the ship was originally christened *Sea Adventure*, the prefix 'Ad' having disappeared through time and usage.

478 **The Castle Island case.**
F. Van Wyck Mason. New York: Reynal & Hitchcock, 1937. 185p.
(Candid Clue Mystery).

One of the better known Bermuda mystery novels. The book is illustrated throughout with black-and-white photographs of well-known actors and local personalities acting out selected scenes from the novel.

Foreign authors in Bermuda

479 Kipling and Bermuda.
Eileen Stamers-Smith. *The Kipling Journal*, vol. 70, no. 277
(March 1996), p. 21-36.
Rudyard Kipling made two trips to Bermuda. From his first trip in February 1894
came the poem, 'That Day', published in 1895, and a letter to the *Spectator*, dated
2 July 1898, in which Kipling presents his theory on how Shakespeare came to write
The Tempest. After his second trip from March to June 1930, he wrote two stories, 'A
Naval Mutiny' (1931) and 'A Sea Dog' (1934), as well as the poem, 'The Coiner'
(1932).

480 Eugene O'Neill and family: the Bermuda interlude.
Joy Bluck Waters. London: Macmillan, 1993. 148p. bibliog.
Eugene O'Neill purchased a home in Bermuda, known as Spithead, in 1926. O'Neill
himself spent little time there but other members of the family continued to visit the
home until it was sold in 1952. Waters' study, first published in Bermuda by the
author in 1992, is based on O'Neill family letters and diaries, and stories from
Bermudians who had contact with the family during their stays on the island. It
includes an account of O'Neill's time spent on Bermuda as well as time spent by the
other members of the family, including O'Neill's daughter Oona, wife of Charlie
Chaplin.

481 Mark Twain and the happy island.
Elizabeth Wallace. New York: Haskell House, 1974. 139p.
Mark Twain made many visits to Bermuda, particularly in the last years of his life.
This book, by someone who knew him in Bermuda during those visits, provides a
glimpse of how he was influenced by Bermuda. Wallace's book was first published in
1913 (Chicago: A. C. McClurg).

482 Tom Moore in Bermuda: a bit of literary gossip.
John Calvin Lawrence Clark. Boston, Massachusetts: Smith &
McCance, 1909. 2nd ed. 63p.
The Irish poet, Tom Moore, arrived in Bermuda in January 1804 to take up the
position of registrar of the court of vice-admiralty. He was not impressed with
Bermuda and so he left in April 1804. Clark chronicles Moore's time in Bermuda and
examines his relationship with Hester Louisa Tucker, wife of St. George's merchant,
William Tucker. Hester was probably the inspiration for Nea of Moore's 'Odes to
Nea, written at Bermuda' which was published in 1806 in *Epistles, odes, and other
poems*. This interesting book is liberally sprinkled with Moore's poetry, as well as
eight black-and-white photographs and eleven black-and-white drawings.

The Arts

Architecture

483 Back to Bermuda.

Penelope Hynam. *City & Country Home*, vol. 10, no. 1 (Feb. 1991), p. 43-71.

Hynam describes four Bermudian homes: Windsong (p. 44-51), originally built in the 17th century and extended in the 19th century; Cragmore (p. 52-59), built at the turn of the 20th century in Greek Revival style; Windfall (p. 60-65), designed by well-known Bermudian architect, Will Onions and built in 1936; and Chelsea (p. 66-71), built in the 1980s for former governor, Sir Edwin and Lady Leather. Colour photographs of all the homes are included. A well-illustrated introduction to the country, 'Bermuda shots', follows Hynam's article (p. 72-77).

484 Wreck House in Bermuda.

Steven M. L. Aronson. *Architectural Digest*, vol. 47, no. 8 (1 Aug. 1990), p. 84-91, 176-78.

Wreck House, built by the Burrows family at the turn of the 19th century in the Georgian Colonial style, is a twelve-room, coral stone house with a traditional limestone roof and Bermudian chimney. The house was formerly owned by film producer, Robert Stigwood, who added two wings to the original structure. Although the article focuses on Stigwood's lifestyle, useful architectural material and nine excellent colour photographs are also included.

485 Architecture: Bermuda style.

David F. Raine. St. George, Bermuda: Pompano Publications, 1989. 2nd ed. 102p.

First published in 1966, this volume traces developments in domestic architecture in Bermuda from the 16th century to the 20th century. Six informative chapters are accompanied by ninety-seven excellent black-and-white photographs. Appendices outline early legislation for the development of Bermuda and list the properties administered by the Bermuda National Trust.

486 The building of Commissioner's House, Bermuda Dockyard.
Jonathan G. Coad. *Post-Medieval Archaeology*, vol. 17 (1983), p. 163-76.

Coad describes the construction of the Commissioner's House between 1822 and 1831. The house, designed by Edward Holl and completed by George Ledwell Taylor, is noted for the extensive use of cast and wrought iron, possibly the first such use in a residential building of this size. Six black-and-white photographs and two architectural plans are included.

487 Bermuda's unique architecture.
Vernon A. Ives. *The Magazine Antiques*, vol. 116, no. 2 (Aug. 1979), p. 341-52.

Although no 17th-century wooden structures survive in Bermuda, a number of early buildings made of native limestone still remain. Ives' discussion of early Bermudian architecture includes detailed descriptions of eight homes built between 1640 and the late 18th century. He also comments on St. Peter's Church (built in 1713), the Old Devonshire Church (built between 1700 and 1720) and Paget Hall (built in 1925), which was heavily influenced by the early homes. Eight colour plates and eleven black-and-white photographs accompany the text.

488 Bermuda cottage plans.
Bermuda Historical Monuments Trust. Hamilton, Bermuda: The Trust, 1948. 54p.

This book of plans, prepared by the Bermuda Historical Monuments Trust, in conjunction with the Department of Works and Health, is designed to assist builders to construct or renovate homes in conformity with Bermudian tradition. In the first section, five Bermudian architects offer floor plans for new houses based on traditional cottage architecture. In the second section, these same architects reproduce the floor plans of six existing Bermuda cottages with suggested alternatives to the interiors to conform with the domestic building requirements which held at the time of writing. Builders and students of architecture will find this item very useful.

489 Bermuda houses.
John S. Humphreys. Boston, Massachusetts: Marshall Jones, 1923. Facsimile edition, edited by Edward C. Harris, Sanders Frith-Brown, Ireland Island, Bermuda: Bermuda Maritime Museum Press, 1993. 321p.

The principal guide to Bermudian domestic architecture. Fourteen pages of introduction and eleven pages of text precede the 181 black-and-white plates which include six floor plans. The aim of the volume is to collect and preserve 'for architects and others interested in small buildings some of the characteristic features and picturesque aspects of the older architecture of the island that are tending to disappear' (Preface).

Festivals

490　**The Bermuda Gombey: Bermuda's unique dance heritage.**
　　　Louise A. Jackson.　Hamilton, Bermuda: Published by the Author,
　　　1987. 28p.

Gombey, pronounced gum-bay, is a parade held on Christmas Eve. Jackson discusses
the various influences – African, West Indian, American Indian, military and Christian
– which apparently contributed to the birth, growth and evolution of this Bermudian
dance form. In addition, she describes the basic movements of the dance and the
rhythms of the music. The book is well illustrated with black-and-white photographs
and drawings of Gombey costumes. The only colour photographs appear on the front
and back covers.

491　**Gombay, a festal rite of Bermudian Negroes.**
　　　H. Carrington Bolton.　*Journal of American Folk-Lore*, vol. 3, no. 10
　　　(July-Sept. 1890), p. 222-26.

Bolton suggests that the roots of Gombay (now Gombey) lie in an ancient African rite
which has been highly modified by a civilized environment. He describes participants
in early Gombey celebrations who dressed in ordinary clothes and wore masks and
headdresses resembling the heads and horns of hideous beasts or imitations of houses
and ships, while playing triangles, tambourines, penny whistles and concertinas. The
lyrics for eight Gombey songs are included.

Furniture

492　**An island's heritage: Bermuda furniture.**
　　　Betsy Kent.　*Art & Antiques*, vol. 5, no. 2 (March-April 1982),
　　　p. 108-15.

Kent summarizes the 17th- and 18th-century styles and techniques used in hand
crafting Bermuda furniture. The early craftsmen learned their trade in the shipbuilding
industry. Their furniture was simple and sturdy, and traditionally made from native
island cedar. She discusses typical Bermudian design characteristics such as
decorative dovetail joints, distinctively shaped aprons, well-turned legs and onion feet.
The article is well illustrated and specific items are described in detail.

493　**Some notes on early Bermudian furniture.**
　　　Colin Cooke, Sylvia Shorto.　*The Magazine Antiques*, vol. 116, no. 2
　　　(Aug. 1979), p. 328-40.

This excellent discussion of 17th- and 18th-century Bermudian furniture contains
useful information about the origins of style, and the techniques and materials used.
There are seven colour plates and twenty-six black-and-white photographs.

494 **Bermuda's antique furniture & silver.**
Bryden Bordley Hyde. Hamilton, Bermuda: Bermuda National Trust,
1971. 198p. map.

This first comprehensive study of Bermudian-made antiques covers the period from
1612 to 1830. Hyde provides some background information (p. 1-10) but the bulk of
the work is given over to a discussion of the furniture (p. 15-153) and the silver
(p. 155-98). This extensive history covers furniture making; individual pieces and the
families and homes they have come from; and the silversmiths and their work. There
are 459 black-and-white photographs and two colour plates.

Music

495 **Curtis: a tribute to Michael Clarke.**
Edited by Dale Butler. Hamilton, Bermuda: The Writers' Machine,
1978. 90p.

This tribute to Charles Michael Clarke (1944-73), a talented and influential Bermudian
singer, guitarist and composer, includes a biography of Clarke and a number of
reminiscences from his friends and fellow performers. *Curtis* is the first of a two-part
record of music in Bermuda (see also following entry).

496 **Jazz on the rock.**
Edited by Dale Butler. Hamilton, Bermuda: The Writers' Machine,
1978. 266p.

Butler's collection of photographs, reminiscences and newspaper articles provides a
brief look at Bermudian musicians, singers, entertainers and dancers. The result is a
good historic record which is not, in fact, restricted to jazz, but also includes big
bands, orchestras, rock and roll, country music and calypso. *Jazz on the rock* is the
second of a two-part record of music in Bermuda (see also preceding entry).

Painting

497 **The imprisoned splendour: the life and work of Sam Morse-Brown.**
David F. Raine. Bridgewater, England: Bigwood & Staple, 1994.
208p.

Sam Morse-Brown was born in 1903 and arrived in Bermuda from Great Britain in the
1970s. His public reputation has been based primarily on his portraiture but he is also
a landscape painter and published poet. This biography, written with Morse-Brown's
assistance, profiles the artist and examines the development of his artistic ideas and
philosophies. Ninety-two black-and-white illustrations accompany the text and

twenty-two colour plates appear in a separate section (p. 193-208). Appendices include a list of twenty portraits commissioned by the National Museum of Wales and twenty portrait drawings in the Imperial War Museum in London. There are also complete lists of Morse-Brown's wartime drawings (1940-48) and portraits produced between 1913 and 1970.

498   The art of Bruce Stuart.
Daniel C. Dempster.   Oakville, Ontario, Canada: Carter & Carter, 1992. 94p.

Contains seventy-five colour reproductions of Bermudian-born Bruce Stuart's paintings. The paintings, representative of work he produced from 1981 to 1991, portray a variety of Bermudian architecture and landscapes: street scenes and backyards, doorways and garden gates, churches, ruins and heritage sites. Also included are Dempster's useful essay entitled 'Introduction: understanding Bruce Stuart' (p. 11-17) and a list of Stuart's exhibitions and awards from 1981 to 1992.

499   Bermudian images: the paintings of Bruce Stuart.
John Adams.   Hamilton, Bermuda: Windjammer Gallery, 1989. 101p.

The fifty colour reproductions of Stuart's paintings included in this volume are highly detailed, almost photographic in nature, and depict individual Bermudian houses or buildings. For each painting, Adams comments on the art work and provides a history of the building.

Photography

500   The beauty of Bermuda.
Scott Stallard, introduction by Peter Benchley.   Toronto: Boulton, Howard & King, 1994. 182p.

Includes 117 colour plates of the most beautiful images from Stallard's first three books (see item nos. 501, 504 and 505), along with a few new photographs, in what he calls 'this final compilation'. In his introduction, novelist Peter Benchley writes that this book 'has captured the essence of Bermuda'.

501   Bermuda: aerial views.
Scott Stallard.   Toronto: Boulton Publishing Services, 1992. 192p.

Stallard's unique views of Bermuda in this collection were all taken from a low-flying helicopter. There are 185 colour plates, each with a one-phrase caption which identifies the subject.

502 **Emeralds on a silver zone: early colour photography in Bermuda 1939-1960.**
Edited by Kevin Stevenson. Hamilton, Bermuda: Bermudian Pub. Co., 1992. 170p.

This unusual collection of 176 colour photographs is largely by amateurs who live in or have spent holidays in Bermuda. Each photograph is captioned and together they provide an historic record of events, people and scenes. The accompanying text by James A. Ziral is a useful addition.

503 **A scape to Bermuda.**
Ian Macdonald-Smith. Paget, Bermuda: Laughing Water, 1991. 138p. 2 maps. bibliog.

Macdonald-Smith's 166 colour plates depict buildings and their architectural details, trees and flowers, landforms and seascapes. Each photograph is accompanied by a title and date. A commentary at the end of the volume (p. 99-138) describes each photograph.

504 **Bermuda II.**
Scott Stallard. Toronto: Boulton Publishing Services, 1990. 183p.

This collection follows directly on the success of Stallard's first book, *Bermuda* (see following entry). *Bermuda II* contains 185 brilliant colour plates, each accompanied by a one-phrase caption. In this work, Stallard emphasizes colour, light and shadows.

505 **Bermuda.**
Scott Stallard. Toronto: Boulton Publishing Services, 1989. 173p.

This is Stallard's first photographic book of Bermuda. The 166 excellent colour plates are each accompanied by short, one-line captions. The great variety of subject matter includes landscapes, seascapes, people, flora and island architecture.

506 **Celebrating the first one hundred years of photography in Bermuda 1839-1939.**
Susanne Notman, edited by Kevin Stevenson. Hamilton, Bermuda: Bermudian Pub. Co., 1989. 169p.

A short (p. 4-8) introductory text precedes the 198 black-and-white photographs which provide a good historical and social chronicle of Bermuda. There are no captions for the photographs, but notes for each appear at the back of the book.

507 **James Bell Heyl: Bermuda's pharmacist-photographer.**
Norman H. Franke. *Pharmacy in History*, vol. 24, no. 3 (1982), p. 117-19.

Heyl, the most important late 19th-century photographer in Bermuda, pursued his career and his love of photography for over fifty years. This brief biography outlines his education in pharmacy in New Orleans, his arrival to practice pharmacy at the Apothecary's Hall in Bermuda in 1846, and touches on his photographic work.

508 **Bermuda abstracts.**
Graeme Outerbridge.   Providence, Rhode Island: Matrix, 1981. 72p. map.

The sixty-two colour photographs in this volume focus on historic homes and architectural features. Outerbridge's photographs turn architectural detail into abstract art. There is no commentary.

Sports

509 **Bermuda National Centre for Youth and Sport.**
Henry Wong, Gene Kinoshita. *Recreation Canada*, special issue
(1985), p. 160-62.
Provides some background to the Bermuda National Centre for Youth and Sport
project and includes a site plan and four elevation diagrams. The design takes into
account the topography of the site and is based on traditional Bermudian architecture.
At the time the article was written the complex had not yet been built. There is a
French translation, 'Centre national de la Jeunesse et des Sports aux Bermudes', on
p. 163.

510 **Bermuda: more than a loafer's paradise.**
David Butwin. *The Physician and Sportsmedicine*, vol. 11, no. 8
(Aug. 1983), p. 166-69.
Butwin outlines a variety of sports available in Bermuda, including snorkelling and
diving, deep-sea fishing, golfing and running.

Food and Drink

511 Bermudian cookery.

Bermuda Junior Service League.   Hamilton, Bermuda: The League, 1995. 10th ed. 192p.

The members of The Bermuda Junior League have gathered together a collection of 320 recipes. Twenty of the recipes come from nine Bermudian restaurants, and fifty-four of the recipes are included in a section devoted to the history of Bermudian cookery. The remainder of the recipes are provided as part of complete menus.

512 All about Bermuda onions.

Nancy Valentine.   Sandys, Bermuda: Hutchings Books, 1991. 2nd ed. 106p.

Valentine gives a history of onions, outlines their health benefits and provides tips on cooking them. The 115 recipes all use the world-famous Bermuda onion, first introduced to Bermuda in 1616, as the main ingredient. There are recipes for soups and salads, breads and muffins, as well as a variety of other dishes.

513 Resort dining in Bermuda.

Richard Sax.   *Bon Appetit*, vol. 36, no. 7 (July 1991), p. 82-91.

Sax describes six Bermudian resorts and their dining establishments, as well as eleven restaurants. He includes four recipes: dark and stormy cocktail; Bermuda fish chowder; scallop and vegetable brochettes; and grilled swordfish with avocado and tomato sauce.

514 The Bermuda cook book.

Cecille C. Snaith-Smith.   Hamilton, Bermuda: Bermuda Press, 1982. 96p.

As well as 119 recipes, Snaith-Smith provides brief histories of some local holiday festivities and food for Christmas, Easter and Guy Fawkes Day. The recipes focus on those foods and dishes most commonly eaten by local families.

515 **What's cooking in Bermuda: a Bermuda cook book of traditional and modern recipes plus interesting background and customs of Bermuda cookery.**
Betsy Ross. Paget, Bermuda: Mrs Douglas Hunter; Printed by Island Press, Hamilton, Bermuda, 1974. rev. ed. 114p.

This popular cookery book was first published in 1957 and has been reprinted frequently. Ross provides 146 recipes for fish dishes, vegetables and fruits, desserts and drinks. These recipes also include dishes for special occasions, such as a Bermudian wedding, Easter, Guy Fawkes Day and Christmas.

Newspapers and Periodicals

Newspapers

516 **Early women journalists: the Stockdales of Bermuda.**
John A. Lent.   In: *Mass communications in the Caribbean.*   John A.
Lent.   Ames, Iowa: Iowa State University Press, 1990, p. 23-30.
Priscilla, Frances and Sarah Stockdale published and edited the *Bermuda Gazette and Weekly Advertiser*, established by their father, Joseph, in 1784, from 1803 to 1816. The newspaper was relinquished to Charles Rollin Beach who married Sarah in 1816. The title was changed to the *Bermuda Gazette and Hamilton and St. George's Weekly Advertiser* in October 1816 and then became the *Bermuda Gazette* in October 1821. The newspaper continued until 1831.

517 **Pioneer women editors – the Stockdale sisters of Bermuda.**
John A. Lent.   *Printing History*, vol. 10, no. 1 (1988), p. 36-39.
This is Lent's original article about the Stockdale family upon which his later chapter (see preceding entry) was based. Here he identifies only two Stockdale sisters, Priscilla and Sarah, and opines that they are 'probably the first women printer-editors in the islands that surround the continental United States' (p. 39). These are two of the points to which Cave (see following entry) objects.

518 **The Stockdale sisters revisited: women printers and editors in the West Indies.**
Roderick Cave.   *Printing History*, vol. 10, no. 2 (1988), p. 38-40.
The purpose of this article is to correct some errors made by John Lent in his 1988 article on the Stockdale sisters (see preceding entry). Cave points out that there were three sisters (Priscilla, Sarah and Frances), not two as Lent had stated, and that they were not the first women printers/editors in the West Indies: Mary Baldwin was editor of the *Weekly Jamaica Courant* from 1722 until the 1730s; and Mrs Browne published *Mrs. Browne's Roseau Gazette and Dominica Chronicle* from 1791 to 1798. In an

untitled rebuttal (p. 40), Lent agrees with the above corrections but denies that he relied solely on secondary sources as Cave implies.

519 The Royal Gazette 1828-1978: a brief history of The Royal Gazette.
Compiled by Marion Robb. Hamilton, Bermuda: Bermuda Press, 1978. 100p.

This brief but detailed history outlines and describes the people and events that shaped the development of *The Royal Gazette* (see item no. 522).

520 Bermuda Sun.
Hamilton, Bermuda: Bermuda Sun Ltd., 1964- . weekly.

This weekly newspaper features mostly general local news with a particularly good section devoted to business reports. It is a tabloid-style, 'independent' newspaper in the sense that it is not affiliated to any political party or platform. The *Bermuda Sun* has the government contract for the *Official Gazette*, as a newspaper of record.

521 Mid-Ocean News.
Hamilton, Bermuda: Bermuda Press, 1911- . weekly.

Features primarily local news and is an 'independent' newspaper. It was originally titled *Mid-Ocean* after its identically named predecessor, which was published from 1899 to 1900, but became *Mid-Ocean News* in 1940. The paper began as a bi-weekly, eventually becoming a daily in 1945. In 1968 it finally established itself as a weekly newspaper.

522 The Royal Gazette.
Hamilton, Bermuda: Royal Gazette Ltd., 1828- . daily.

Bermuda's leading newspaper, an 'independent' which is published daily from Monday to Saturday, provides a comprehensive mix of international and local news. The newspaper began as a weekly and eventually achieved daily status in 1921.

Periodicals

523 Bermudian Business.
Hamilton, Bermuda: Bermudian Pub. Co., 1996- . quarterly.

This glossy quarterly deals primarily with banking and the insurance industry but is also a useful source for those conducting business in Bermuda. Several feature articles in each issue supplement the regular business columns.

524 **Bermuda Magazine.**
Hamilton, Bermuda: Bermuda Marketing Ltd., 1993- . quarterly.

This well-illustrated, glossy quarterly contains several informative and entertaining articles in each issue. There are also regular columns on nature, books, and arts and crafts.

525 **Bermuda Journal of Archaeology and Maritime History.**
Mangrove Bay, Bermuda: Bermuda Maritime Museum, 1989- . annual.

Aimed at continuing and expanding the role of the *Bermuda Historical Quarterly* (see item no. 528). With the demise of that journal in 1981, there had been no medium for the publication of Bermudian historical research. Articles appearing in this journal have been indexed in *Bermuda in print* (see item no. 539).

526 **Bermuda Maritime Museum Quarterly.**
Mangrove Bay, Bermuda: Bermuda Maritime Museum, 1988- . quarterly.

This journal continues two other publications, the *Bulletin of the Institute of Maritime History and Archaeology* and *Ratlines*, both of which had been issued by the Bermuda Maritime Museum. The *Quarterly* is designed to present information on all aspects of the operation of the Museum.

527 **Bermuda Educational Journal.**
Hamilton, Bermuda: Amalgamated Bermuda Union of Teachers, 1984- . irregular.

The Bermuda Union of Teachers was established in 1919 and began publishing the *Bermuda Educational Journal* as an annual in 1941. It was short-lived. In 1964 the Bermuda Union of Teachers joined with the Teachers' Association of Bermuda to form the Amalgamated Bermuda Union of Teachers. The present journal contains articles and creative writing by union members.

528 **Bermuda Historical Quarterly.**
Hamilton, Bermuda: Bermuda Historical Society, 1944-81. quarterly.

The *Bermuda Historical Quarterly* was originally intended to 'include original articles, private letters and other papers when available and extracts from the Archives of Bermuda. There will also be an attempt to note any development in our contemporary life which appears to be of permanent historical interest' (no. 1, 1944, p. 2). The journal published contributed articles and transcripts of the Minutes of Council from 1684 to 1756. This practice has been continued by the *Bermuda Journal of Archaeology and Maritime History* (see item no. 525). There is no published index for the journal but individual articles are indexed in *Bermuda in print* (see item no. 539) and the Bermuda Library has produced an index for in-house use.

529   **Bermudian Magazine.**
Hamilton, Bermuda: Bermudian Pub. Co., 1930- . monthly.

This glossy monthly is produced for residents and tourists. Each issue contains several feature articles on Bermudian topics. In addition, there are regular columns dealing with real estate, social events, food, topical commentary, and a list of births, marriages and deaths.

Libraries and Archives

530 **A guide to the records of Bermuda.**
Helen Rowe. Hamilton, Bermuda: The Bermuda Archives, 1980.
132p. map. bibliog.

Lists records in Bermuda as well as Bermuda-related materials in foreign repositories. The Bermuda records can be found in the Bermuda Archives, various government departments, several schools and historical societies, and the Maritime Museum. The foreign repositories are located in the United Kingdom and Northern Ireland, Ireland, the United States, Canada, Spain, the Bahamas, Barbados and Jamaica.

531 **The Bermuda Library: of books, and blooms, and little white devils.**
Gary Thomson. *Wilson Library Bulletin*, vol. 53, no. 10 (June 1979), p. 700-03.

Thomson outlines the history of the Bermuda Library which was founded in 1839 and originally housed in the Governor's Room in the Colonial Secretariat. In 1916 the library was moved to Par-la-Ville, an estate house built in 1843. The library is still situated there, though the property was renovated and enlarged in 1957, and also includes the Bermuda Historical Monuments Trust Archives and the Bermuda Historical Society Museum. Thomson also describes two branch libraries: the St. George's Branch Library, opened in 1951; and the Somerset Branch, opened in 1957. Unfortunately, these two branches were closed in the early 1990s.

532 **Guide to libraries and archives in Central America and the West Indies, Panama, Bermuda, and British Guiana, supplemented with information on private libraries, bookbinding, bookselling and printing.**
Arthur Eric Gropp.   New Orleans, Louisiana: Middle American Research Institute, Tulane University of Louisiana, 1941. 721p. map. bibliog. (Tulane University of Louisiana. Middle American Research Institute. Middle American Research Series. Publication, no. 10).

In February 1938, Gropp spent fifteen days in Bermuda visiting libraries (public, private and rental), archives, booksellers and printers as part of the Middle American Research Institute's survey of libraries and archives in Central America, the West Indies and Bermuda. Although now quite out of date, the section on Bermuda (p. 191-211) provides a good overview of the prewar situation in the country. This work also allows for comparison between Bermuda and what were then other British colonies in the Caribbean. Gropp offers good descriptions of archival holdings and the libraries he visited, particularly the Public Library in Hamilton and the St. George's Historical Library.

533 **The libraries of Bermuda, the Bahamas, the British West Indies, British Guiana, British Honduras, Puerto Rico, and the American Virgin Islands: a report to the Carnegie Corporation of New York.**
Ernest A. Savage.   London: Library Association, 1934. 103p.

Savage spent one day in Bermuda during a ten-week tour of libraries in the Caribbean. The section on Bermuda (p. 3-5) provides information on the Hamilton Public Library, founded in 1839, several school libraries, and a special library devoted to law. Savage's recommendations, which apply to the Caribbean as a whole and to the individual islands he visited, pertain to library legislation, finance, library staffs and joint administration. Though now out of date, the report is useful for research purposes.

Directories

534 **Bermuda Business Pages: Bermuda's Guide to Local Business.**
Edited by Kevin Stevenson.   Hamilton, Bermuda: Bermudian Pub.
Co., 1994- . annual.

Lists domestic businesses by business type. For each business, the directory entry gives the name, location address, postal address, telephone and fax numbers, days and hours of operation, names of senior personnel, nature of the business and services provided.

535 **Bermuda Business Directory.**
Edited by Kevin Stevenson.   Hamilton, Bermuda: Bermudian Pub.
Co., 1991- . bi-annual.

This directory provides two major lists: Bermuda companies; and professional associations and government bodies. For each company, the directory entry gives the location address, postal address, telephone and fax numbers, year established, names of the partners, number of employees and services provided. For each professional association, the entry indicates the address, telephone and fax numbers, a list of officers, a history of the association and its objectives. *Bermuda Business Directory* continues *Bermuda Directory* which was first published in 1989.

536 **Who's who in Bermuda 1982-85.**
Warwick, Bermuda: J. B. Enterprises, 1987. 2nd ed. 228p.

A general, alphabetical directory containing biographies and some black-and-white photographs. There are also separate lists of such notables as Governors of Bermuda, 1612- ; Bishops of Bermuda, 1925- ; Chief Justices of Bermuda, 1684- ; House of Assembly Speakers, 1622- ; current government members; Mayors of Hamilton, 1795- and St. George, 1797- ; and Miss Bermuda Beauty Queens, 1965- . The first edition, *Who's who in Bermuda 1980-81*, was published privately in 1982. There is no indication of any further editions beyond the second.

537 **Dictionary of Latin American and Caribbean biography.**
Edited by Ernest Kay. Ely, England: Melrose Press, 1971. 2nd ed.
458p.

This 'who's who' provides one alphabetic sequence of individuals by surname. There is no geographical information although the foreword indicates that individuals from Bermuda are included. The first edition was published in 1969 under the title *Dictionary of Caribbean biography*.

538 **Personalities Caribbean: the International Guide to Who's Who in the West Indies, Bahamas, Bermuda.**
Kingston, Jamaica: Personalities, 1965- . irregular.

A straightforward 'who's who' which appears on an irregular basis. The majority of entries for Bermuda come from politics, government and business, though there are also entries for individuals from law, religion, medicine and education. Some entries are accompanied by black-and-white photographic portraits. This work continues *Personalities in the Caribbean* which was first published in 1962.

Bibliographies

539   **Bermuda in print: a guide to the printed literature on Bermuda.**
Archibald Cameron Hollis Hallett.   Pembroke, Bermuda: Juniperhill
Press, 1995. 2nd ed. 325p.

This bibliography, which was first published in 1985 (Hamilton, Bermuda: IPL),
contains over 2,000 unnumbered entries listed alphabetically by author. There is also a
classified subject list. For each entry, Hallett gives the author and title of the item; the
place of publication, the publisher and the date of publication; the collation and size of
the item in centimetres; the Library of Congress classification number; and, in some
cases, a brief annotation. There are several exclusions: government documents; all
works of fiction for which Bermuda is the setting; cookery books; and most
specialized scientific papers. Despite this, the bibliography is most useful. Hallett has
included sections on Bermudian newspapers, almanacs and periodicals as well as the
history of printing and publishing in Bermuda. All articles from the *Bermuda
Historical Quarterly* (1944-81), the *Bermuda Journal of Archaeology and Maritime
History* (1989-93), and *Heritage* (1980-88) have been listed in this bibliography.

540   **The Bermuda national bibliography.**
Bermuda Library.   Hamilton, Bermuda: The Library, 1983- . annual.

Includes works about Bermuda and Bermudians published locally and abroad; works
published in Bermuda on other subjects; and works published abroad by Bermudians. The
bibliography lists monographs, periodical publications, published and unpublished
government reports, and other reports and maps. The entries are listed in classified
order by the Dewey Decimal Classification System. There is an index of authors, titles
and series.

541   **Bermuda Triangle bibliography.**
Larry Kusche, Deborah K. Blouin.   Tempe, Arizona: University
Library, Arizona State University, 1975. 3rd ed. 9p.
This slight bibliography contains references to 223 items including books and book
chapters, periodical and newspaper articles, government reports and films. There are
no annotations.

542   **The Bermuda Triangle: an annotated bibliography.**
Carol F. Stancil.   Los Angeles, California: Reference Section, College
Library, UCLA, 1973. 10p.
Stancil lists and annotates only forty-four items, explaining that the bibliography is
not exhaustive but is the best of the essential information to date. The list includes
books, periodical and newspaper articles, and government publications.

543   **Bermudiana bibliography.**
Bermuda Library.   Hamilton, Bermuda: The Library, 1971. 27p. map.
The preface to this bibliography states that it is 'intended as an introduction and guide
to the special collection of Bermudiana which is housed in the Reference Department
of the Bermuda Library'. Not all items in the collection are listed and there is no
indication why some are missing. However, the bibliography, a precursor to the
Bermuda national bibliography (see item no. 540), does list, without annotations, 213
items in 31 separate subject areas.

544   **Bermuda in periodical literature: a bibliography.**
George Watson Cole.   Brookline, Massachusetts: Riverdale Press,
1907. 275p.
Cole's bibliography originally appeared in two series in the *Bulletin of Bibliography*.
The first preliminary list, which was also published as a separate item (see item no.
545), appeared in volume 1, p. 52-54, 74-76. The second series, which included the
items from volume 1, appeared in twenty-six numbers of the *Bulletin of Bibliography*
from October 1900 (vol. 2, no. 5) to January 1907 (vol. 4, no. 10). The 1,382 entries
are listed alphabetically by journal title, then alphabetically by author. Interestingly,
the bibliography also contains references to books listed alphabetically by author. The
work contains the main bibliography plus an addenda and a post-addenda. There is
also a miscellaneous section in which Cole has listed those items he has been unable
to examine or verify.

545   **Bermuda in periodical literature: a bibliography.**
George Watson Cole.   Boston, Massachusetts: Boston Book Co.,
1898. 25p. (*Bulletin of Bibliography*, no. 2).
A list of 145 periodical articles on Bermuda. The articles are primarily in English,
though there are some in French, German, Swedish and Spanish. They are listed
alphabetically by periodical title. Topics include science and natural history, creative
writing, architecture, history and archaeology, description and travel accounts,
bibliography and law.

Index

The index is a single alphabetical sequence of authors (personal and corporate), titles of publications and subjects. Index entries refer both to the main items and to other works mentioned in the notes to each item. Title entries are in italics. Numeration refers to the items as numbered.

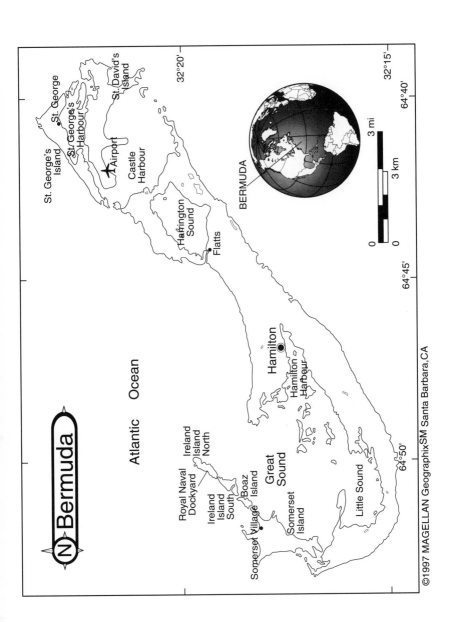

N

Bermuda

Atlantic   Ocean

St. George's Island

St. George

St. George's Harbour

St. George's Island

Airport

Castle Harbour

St. David's Island

32°20'

Harrington Sound

Flatts

Hamilton

Hamilton Harbour

Royal Naval Dockyard

Ireland Island North

Ireland Island South

Boaz Island

Somerset Village

Somerset Island

Great Sound

Little Sound

BERMUDA

64°45'

64°50'

32°15'

64°40'

3 mi

3 km

0

0

©1997 MAGELLAN GeographixSM Santa Barbara,CA

ALSO FROM CLIO PRESS

INTERNATIONAL ORGANIZATIONS SERIES

Each volume in the International Organizations Series is either devoted to one specific organization, or to a number of different organizations operating in a particular region, or engaged in a specific field of activity. The scope of the series is wide-ranging and includes intergovernmental organizations, international non-governmental organizations, and national bodies dealing with international issues. The series is aimed mainly at the English-speaker and each volume provides a selective, annotated, critical bibliography of the organization, or organizations, concerned. The bibliographies cover books, articles, pamphlets, directories, databases and theses and, wherever possible, attention is focused on material about the organizations rather than on the organizations' own publications. Notwithstanding this, the most important official publications, and guides to those publications, will be included. The views expressed in individual volumes, however, are not necessarily those of the publishers.

VOLUMES IN THE SERIES